D0202395

Mozart

Mozart

Portrait of a Genius

NORBERT ELIAS

Edited by
Michael Schröter

Translated by
Edmund Jephcott

University of California Press
Berkeley and California

University of California Press
Berkeley and Los Angeles, California

Cataloging-in-publication data are available from the Library of Congress.

Library of Congress Catalog Card Number: 93–60280

ISBN: 0–520–08475–6

Typeset in 11 on 12½ pt Plantin
by Times Graphics, Singapore
Printed and bound in Great Britain by
Biddles Ltd, Guildford and King's Lynn

This book is printed on acid-free paper

Contents

The quotations from *The Letters of Mozart and his Family* translated by Emily Anderson are reprinted by kind permission of Macmillan Press Ltd.

PART I

Sociological Reflections on Mozart

He Simply Gave Up and Let Go

Wolfgang Amadeus Mozart died in 1791, aged thirty five, and was buried in a pauper's grave on 6 December. Whatever the acute illness that contributed to his early decease may have been, Mozart was often close to despair in the period before his death. He slowly began to feel himself a man defeated by life. His debts mounted. His family moved from one lodging to another. Success in Vienna, which perhaps meant more to him than any other, failed to materialise. Viennese high society turned its back on him. The rapid advance of his fatal illness may well have had to do with the fact that his life had lost its value for him. He clearly died with the sense that his social existence was a failure; metaphorically speaking, he died of the meaninglessness of his life, his complete loss of the belief that his deepest wish would be fulfilled. Two sources of his will to live, two springs that fed his sense of his own value and meaning, had almost dried up: the love of a woman he could trust for him, and the love of the Viennese public for his music. For a time he had enjoyed both; and both held the highest place in the hierarchy of his wishes. There is much reason to believe that in the last years of his life he increasingly felt that he had lost both. That was his tragedy and ours, as human beings.

Nowadays, when the mere name of Mozart has become for many people a symbol of the highest musical delight known to our world, it might well seem incomprehensible that a man possessed of such magical powers of creativity could have met a premature death, and taken who knows what unborn musical creations with him to the grave, because the withholding of favour and love by other people had deepened his doubt in the value and meaning of his life. This can be especially hard to believe if one is interested only in his work, and not in the person who created it. But in thinking about such connections one should not be misled into judging the meaning or meaninglessness of someone else's life by the standard one may apply to one's own. One must ask what that other person regarded as fulfilment, or felt as the emptiness of his or her life. Mozart himself was well aware of his unusual gift, and had passed on as much of it as he could. He had worked tirelessly for much of his life. It would be rash to assert that he was unaware that his music would go down to posterity. But he was not the kind of person to be consoled by the thought of the recognition his work would find in future generations for the lack of recognition he had to endure in the last years of his life, especially in his adoptive city, Vienna. Posthumous fame meant relatively little to him – present fame everything. He had fought for it in full awareness of his own worth. But, as happens so often, he needed direct confirmation of his worth by others, especially his close friends and acquaintances. He was finally deserted by most of those who had earlier been closest to him. That was not only their fault – matters were not as straightforward as that. But there is no doubt that his loneliness grew. Perhaps in the end he simply gave up and let go. 'Mozart's late but rapid decline', one of his biographers writes, 'after long periods of intensive work rarely interrupted by illness or indisposition; his brief, almost breathless act of dying, his sudden death after a coma of only two hours – all his seems to demand a better explanation than the one furnished by traditional medicine.'[1]

There is, moreover, strong evidence that Mozart was tormented by increasing doubts about the affection and even the fidelity of his Constanze, whom he loved in spite of everything. His wife's second husband later reported that she had always had more respect for his talent than for his person.[2] However, her perception of his talent seems to have depended less on her understanding of his music than of its success. When this declined, when the Viennese court, previously his patron, dropped this uncompromising artist in favour of shallower composers, Constanze's regard for his talent was no doubt shaken like that for his person. The increasing impoverishment of his family that went with the declining appreciation of his music at the end of Mozart's life may have further cooled his wife's never deep feelings for him. Thus the two factors that deprived his life of meaning, the loss of favour with the public and the ebbing of his wife's affection, were not unconnected. They were two inseparable, interdependent strata in the feeling of meaninglessness that overtook him in his last years.

On the other hand, Mozart was a person who felt an insatiable need for love, both physical and emotional. It is one of the secrets of his life that he probably suffered, from his earliest years, from the feeling that nobody loved him. Much in his music may well be a constant courting of affection, the wooing of favour by a man who from childhood had never been quite sure that he deserved the love of others that meant so much to him, and who may in some respects have felt little love for himself. The word 'tragedy' may sound somewhat platitudinous and grandiose in this connection. Nevertheless, it can be said with some justice that the tragic side of Mozart's existence was that he,

---

1 Wolfgang Hildesheimer, *Mozart*, (trans. by Marion Faber), London/Toronto/Melbourne 1983, p. 355.
2 Quoted by Hildesheimer, *Mozart*, p. 244.

who had striven so hard to win people's love, should have felt while still young, as he did at the end of his life, that he was no longer loved by anyone, not even himself. That is undoubtedly the kind of meaninglessness that someone can die of. At the end, it seems, Mozart was in a state of loneliness and despair. He really knew that he was soon to die, and in his case that must have meant that he also wished to die, and that in large measure he wrote the *Requiem* for himself.

How reliable the pictures are that we have of Mozart, especially the young Mozart, is an open question. But one of the traits that make him more appealing, or, if you will, more human, is that he did not have one of those heroic faces, like the better-known physiognomies of Goethe or Beethoven, which marked their owners out as men of genius as soon as they entered a room or set foot in the street. Mozart's face was not heroic at all. The prominent, fleshy nose, which seemed to bend to meet the slightly upturned chin, lost something of its hugeness as the face filled out. The very alert, lively eyes, at once mischievous and dreamy, look out above it – still somewhat sheepishly in the young man of twenty-four in the family portrait by Johann Nepomuk della Croce;[3] more self-confidently, but still with the dreamy, roguish look, in later portraits. The pictures show a little of a side of Mozart that is readily lost to view in the selection of his works dictated by the taste of the concert-going public, yet which deserves mention if we are to bring Mozart to life as a man. It is the joker in him, the clown who jumps over chairs and tables, turns somersaults and plays games with words and, of course, with sounds. We should not understand Mozart fully if we forgot that there were hidden corners of his personality that are best characterised by the later injunction 'Lache, Bajazzo' (Laugh, Clown), or the memory of the unloved and deceived Petrushka.

3   Cf. the reproduction in Hildesheimer, *op. cit.*, following p. 152.

After his death his wife said she felt 'pity' for the 'deceived' Mozart.[4] It is very unlikely that she did not 'deceive' him (if the word is appropriate at all) or that he did not know – just as it is unlikely that he entirely abstained from similar conduct with other women. But this applies to the later years, when the lights were slowly going out in his life, when the feeling of being unloved, a failure, that is, the ever-present depressive tendency in him, came closer to the surface under the weight of professional setbacks and domestic woe. At that time the discrepancy which is so striking in Mozart came into the open: the discrepancy between his eminently meaningful social life seen objectively, more precisely from a he-perspective, and the increasingly meaningless life he led from an I-perspective, that is from the standpoint of his own feelings.

To begin with, things had gone well for a number of years. The strict discipline imposed by his father paid off. It was converted into the self-discipline that enabled the young man as he worked to cleanse the confused dreams seething within him of their personal dross and transform them into public music without any loss of spontaneity or inventiveness. All the same, Mozart had to pay a high price for the great benefit he gained from the ability to objectify his personal fantasies.

To understand a person, one needs to know the primordial wishes he or she longs to fulfil. Whether or not people's lives make sense to them depends on whether or how far they are able to realise these wishes. But they are not embedded in advance of all experience. They evolve from early childhood in life with other people, and are fixed gradually, over the years, in the form that will determine the course of life; sometimes, however, this will happen suddenly, in conjunction with an especially momentous experience. Undoubtedly, people are often unaware of these dominant, guiding wishes as such. Nor does it ever depend entirely on them whether or how far the wishes are fulfilled,

---

4 Hildesheimer, *op. cit.*, p. 244.

since they are always directed towards others, the social nexus people form together. Almost all people have definite wishes that are capable of being fulfilled; almost all have some deeper wishes that are simply unfulfillable, at least at the present stage of knowledge.

In Mozart's case these latter wishes, too, can be detected; and they are responsible in no small measure for the tragic course of his life. We have stereotyped technical terms to denote the aspects of his character alluded to by this statement. We could speak, for example, of a manic-depressive personality structure with paranoid features; its depressive tendencies would have been kept in check for a time by the subject's ability to harness musical daydreaming in a reality-orientated way and the resulting success; but then the self-destructive tendencies, particularly those fighting against success in love and social life, gained the upper hand. Admittedly, the special form such tendencies took in Mozart's case suggests that a somewhat different idiom might be needed.

It does indeed appear to be the case that Mozart, proud as he was of himself and his gifts, had no love of himself at the bottom of his heart; and it is quite conceivable that he did not find himself particularly lovable. His appearance was not attractive. At first sight his face was unprepossessing; possibly he wished for a different face when he looked into the mirror. The vicious circle inherent in such a situation arises from the fact that a person's face and physique may fall short of their wishes and arouse dislike partly because something of their guilt feelings, of their secret aversion to themselves, finds expression in them. Whatever the reasons may have been, in the later years when his outward situation was deteriorating Mozart's sense of not being loved clearly emerged more sharply, together with an equally strong, unfulfilled desire to be loved, on several planes – by his wife, by other women, by other people in general, that is, to be loved both as a man and as a musician. His immense ability to dream in sound-structures served this secret coveting of love and affection.

Of course, the dreaming in sound patterns was also an end in itself. The rich abundance of his musical imagination dispelled for a time, it seems, his grief over his lack or loss of love. It may have suppressed his constant suspicion that his wife's love had gone to other men, and his gnawing sense of being not quite worthy of the love of others – a feeling which played its part in turning the love and affection of others away from him, and causing his great success to be short-lived, to vanish quite soon like a chimera.

The tragedy of Bajazzo is only an image. But it goes some way towards clarifying the connection between Mozart the buffoon and the great artist, between the eternal child and the creative man, between Papageno's tomfoolery and the deep seriousness of Pamina's longing for death. That a man may be a great artist does not prevent him from being something of a clown; that he was really a winner, and was certainly a gain for humanity, does not prevent him from seeing himself as a loser, and thereby condemning himself to be a loser in reality.

Mozart's tragedy, which was partly of this kind, is all too easily hidden from later listeners by the enchanting quality of his music. This dulls our involvement with him. It cannot be quite right to separate the artist from the man retrospectively in this way. It may be difficult, after all, to love Mozart's art without feeling a little love for the man who created it.

Bourgeois Musicians in Court Society

Mozart emerges vividly as a human being only if his wishes are seen in the context of his time. His life is a case study of a situation the peculiarity of which often escapes us, since we are used to operating with static concepts. Was Mozart, we tend to ask, a musical representative of rococo or of the bourgeois nineteenth century? Was his work the last manifestation of a pre-Romantic 'objective' music, or does it already show signs of the rising 'subjectivism'?

The trouble is that such categories do not take us much further. They are academic abstractions that do not do justice to the process-character of the observable social data to which they refer. Underlying them is the idea that the tidy division into epochs we usually find in history books best fits the actual course of social development. Each figure who is known through the magnitude of his or her achievement is then allocated to one epoch or the other as its high point. On closer examination, however, it not uncommonly emerges that outstanding achievements occur most frequently at times which could at most be called transitional phases if static concepts of epochs are used. In other words, such achievements arise from the dynamics of the conflict between the canons of older declining classes and newer rising ones.

This is certainly true of Mozart. The aim of his wishes, and the reasons why – contrary to the judgement of posterity – he felt like a failure at the end of his life, cannot be properly understood if this conflict of standards is left out of account. For the conflict was not played out only in the broad social field, between the values and ideals of courtly aristocratic classes and those of bourgeois strata; things were not so simple. It was played out also within many individual people, including Mozart himself, as a conflict running through their entire social existence.

Mozart's life very graphically illustrates the situation of bourgeois groups who were dependent outsiders in an economy dominated by the court aristocracy at a time when the power balance still strongly favoured the court establishment, but not so strongly as to suppress all expressions of protest, at least in the politically less dangerous arena of culture. As a bourgeois outsider in service to the court Mozart fought with astonishing courage to free himself from his aristocratic patrons and masters. He did so with his own resources, for the sake of his personal dignity and his musical work. And he lost the battle – as, one might add with the presumption of hindsight, was only to be expected. Here as in other cases, however, this presumption obscures the structure of what we now call 'history'. It also blocks our understanding of the meaning the course of events in an earlier time had for its human representatives themselves.

I have said something about the structure of the conflict of canons between court and bourgeois groups in a different context.[1] I have tried to demonstrate that in the second half of the eighteenth century concepts like 'civility' or 'civilisation' on one hand and 'culture' on the other were used in Germany as symbols of different canons of behaviour and feeling. It was possible to show that the use of these words reflected the chronic tension between court establishment circles and bourgeois outsider groups. This also highlighted certain aspects of the bitter class struggles between the

1 Norbert Elias, *State Formation and Civilization*, Oxford 1982, Ch. 1.

middle classes and the aristocracy (which go back as far as the origins of the medieval towns in Europe). Like the structure of European societies, the social character of the two groups changed in a specific way during their seven or eight centuries of struggle – a struggle that finally came to an end in the twentieth century with the rise of the two economic classes and the de-functionalisation of the nobility as a social stratum. Conflicts between different canons, as well as a drawing together and merging of the standards of bourgeois and noble groups, can be observed throughout this long class struggle. It was the soil from which aristocratic absolutism grew,[2] just as the bourgeois and proletarian absolutism of our day has arisen from the struggles between these two economic strata.

But so far we lack not only an overall study of the course and structure of the long class conflict between the nobility and the bourgeoisie in European (or other) societies; we also lack studies of many individual aspects of the social tensions that concern us here. Mozart's life illustrates one of these aspects in a truly paradigmatic way – the fate of a bourgeois person in court service towards the end of the period when, almost everywhere in Europe, the taste of the court nobility set the standard for artists of all social origins, in keeping with the general distribution of power. This applied especially to music and architecture.

In the fields of literature and philosophy it was possible, in Germany in the second half of the eighteenth century, to liberate oneself from the court–aristocratic canon of taste. People working in these sectors could reach their audience through books; and as there was a fairly large and growing reading public among the bourgeoisie in Germany in this period, class-specific cultural forms were able to emerge relatively early there. These forms matched the canon of taste of non-courtly, bourgeois groups, and expressed their

---

2 Cf. Norbert Elias, *The Court Society*, Oxford 1983.

growing confidence in face of the dominant aristocratic establishment.

With regard to music the situation was still quite different at that time – especially in Austria and its capital Vienna, the seat of the imperial court, but generally in the smaller German countries as well. In Germany as in France the people working in this field were still heavily dependent on the favour, the patronage and thus the taste of court and aristocratic circles (and of the urban bourgeois patriciate which followed their example). Indeed, even for Mozart's generation, a musician who wanted to be socially recognised as a serious artist and at the same time to feed himself and his family, had to find a position within the network of court institutions and their offshoots. He had no choice. If he felt within him a vocation that would lead to outstanding achievements, whether as performer or as composer, it was practically taken for granted that he could only reach his goal by finding a permanent appointment at a court, preferably a rich and splendid one. In Protestant countries the position of church organist and conductor in one of the large, semi-autonomous towns, usually ruled by a patrician group, was open to him as well. But even there, as we can see from the life of Telemann, for example, it was an advantage in seeking a post as a professional musician to have previously held a similar office at court.

What we call the princely court was essentially the prince's household. Musicians were just as indispensable at such large households as pastry cooks, cooks and valets, and usually had about the same status in the court hierarchy. They were what are somewhat contemptuously called court flunkeys. Most musicians were no doubt satisfied with being provided for, like the other middle-class people at court. Among those who were not satisfied was Mozart's own father. But he too bowed, unwillingly, to circumstances he could not escape.

This was the fixed framework within which each individual musical talent had to express itself. It is hardly possible to understand the music of that time, its 'style' as it is often called, without this framework clearly in view. We shall come back to this later.

Mozart's individual fate, his destiny as a unique human being and thus also a unique artist, was heavily influenced by his social situation, the dependence of a musician of his time on the court aristocracy. We can see here how difficult it is to elucidate – as a biographer, for example, tries to do – the problems individuals encounter in their lives, no matter how incomparable an individual's personality or achievements may be, unless one has mastered the craft of the sociologist.[3] One needs to be able to draw a clear picture of the social pressures acting on the individual. Such a study is not a historical narrative but the elaboration of a verifiable theoretical model of the figuration which a person – in this case an eighteenth-century artist – formed through his interdependence with other social figures of his time.

How the twenty-one-year-old Mozart asked to be released by his employer, the prince-bishop of Salzburg, in 1777 (after his request for a vacation had been refused), how he then set off fresh, happy and full of hope to seek a position at the Munich court, with the patricians of Augsburg, in Mannheim and Paris, where he waited in vain, an increasingly embittered man, in the antechambers of influential ladies and gentlemen of the nobility, how he finally returned unwilling and disappointed to Salzburg to be appointed leader of the orchestra and court organist – all that is well enough known. But the significance of this experience for Mozart's personal development – and so for his development as a musician or, to put it differently, for that of his music – cannot be convincingly and realistically assessed if

---

3 Sociology is usually regarded as a destructive, reductive discipline. I do not share this view. For me sociology is a science that ought to help us understand better, and explain, what is incomprehensible in our social life. This is why I have chosen the seemingly paradoxical subtitle 'The sociology of a genius'. It is not my purpose to destroy genius or reduce it to something else, but to make its human situation easier to understand, and perhaps help in some small way to answer the question of what should be done to prevent a fate like Mozart's from happening. By presenting his tragedy as I try to do – and it is only an example of a more general problem – it may be possible to make people more aware of the need to behave more considerately towards innovators.

one merely describes the fate of the individual person, without also offering a model of the social structures of his time, especially where they led to differences of power. Only within the framework of such a model can one discern what a person like Mozart enmeshed in this society was able to do as an individual, and what – no matter how strong, great or unique he may have been – he was not able to do. Only then, in short, can one understand the inescapable compulsions acting on Mozart and how he behaved in relation to them, whether he bowed to their pressure and was thereby influenced in his musical production, or whether he tried to escape or even oppose them.

Not the least of the reasons for Mozart's tragedy was the fact that he tried, both personally and in his work, to break through the barriers of the social power structure by his own individual efforts, while still being strongly tied to his society's taste by his musical imagination and his musical conscience – and that he did so in a phase of social development when the traditional power structure was virtually intact.

Most people who took up a musical career were non-noble by social origin, or, in our terminology, bourgeois. If they wanted to be successful within court society, and to find opportunities to develop their talents as performers or composers, they were obliged by their lowly position to adopt the court canon of behaviour and feeling not only in their musical taste but in their dress and their whole make-up as people. In our day this need to adapt to the demands of an establishment is more or less taken for granted by socially dependent people, in keeping with the distribution of power. The employees of a large concern or department store, especially if they are interested in promotion, soon learn how to adjust their behaviour to the canon of the establishment. However, the power difference between economic establishments and outsiders in societies where there is a fairly free market for supply and demand and even, in some areas, for professional appointments, is much less than that between absolute rulers or their councillors and their court musicians – even though artists who were famous and *à la mode* could take some liberties. The famous Gluck, a man of petty-bourgeois origin who absorbed the subtleties of the ruling canon with great verve both in his musical taste and in his personal behaviour, could, like every other courtly man, get away with quite a lot, including uncouth behaviour. There was thus not only a court nobility but a court bourgeoisie.

Up to a point Mozart's father belonged to this class. He was an employee, or more precisely a civil servant, of the archbishop of Salzburg, who at that time was naturally a ruling prince, in a petty state. Like all rulers of his kind the archbishop had, if on a reduced scale, the whole official apparatus that was part and parcel of an absolutist court, including an orchestra. Leopold Mozart was deputy conductor. Such offices were filled and paid in much the same way as those of employees in a private firm in the 19th century. The signs of subordinate status expected of court employees were probably even more demonstrative, given the greater power difference, as were the rulers' taken-for-granted gestures of superiority.[4]

Perhaps one should add that the relationships between rulers and servants – even middle-ranking ones like Leopold Mozart – were far more personal, even at the imperial court in Vienna and certainly at the petty court of the archbishop of Salzburg, than between the directors and middle management in a large commercial enterprise of our day. As a rule the princes themselves decided on appointments to their orchestras. The social distance was immense, but the spatial distance very small. People were always close together, the master always at hand.

While the normal social situation of a musician in Mozart's lifetime was that of a servant at court, where he

4 For similar reasons, the duties to be performed were less specialised. When Bach was appointed organist at the Weimar court of the very pious Duke Wilhelm-Ernst, he also had to put on a border guard's uniform and play his fiddle in the small chamber orchestra.

took orders from a powerful individual higher up in the hierarchy, there were nevertheless exceptions within this society. Individual musicians could so please the court public by their special talent as virtuoso or composer that their fame spread beyond the local court where they were employed to the highest levels of society. In such cases a bourgeois muscian might be treated almost as an equal by court nobles. He was invited, as happened with Mozart, to the courts of the mighty to perform; emperors and kings openly expressed their enjoyment of his art and their admiration for his achievements. He was allowed to dine at their tables – usually in exchange for a piano performance; he frequently stayed at their houses when on his travels, and was thus intimately acquainted with their style of life and their taste.

It was characteristic of a great court-bourgeois artist that he lived to an extent in two worlds. Mozart's whole life and work were marked by this split.[5] On one hand he moved in aristocratic court circles whose musical taste he had adopted and whose canon of behaviour he was expected to follow. On the other he represented a specific type of what we are obliged to denote by far too coarse a term as the 'petty bourgeoisie' of his time. He was a member of the circle of middle-rank court employees, what might be called the world 'below stairs'.[6] In England the dominant canon of behaviour and feeling was largely and characteristically transferred to the personnel of the aristocratic household

5 The split is certainly not only characteristic of Mozart; it and its influence on personal make-up are found in other bourgeois artists and intellectuals in court society. A well-known example of this occurred when Voltaire challenged a high-born noble by whom he felt insulted to a duel, and the noble had him thrashed by one of his lackeys in the street, as a sign that he regarded the challenge from a bourgeois as arrogance. The fact that people from the bourgeois class who were distinguished by a special artistic or intellectual talent were received almost as equals in some Paris *salons* and by some German and Italian nobles, can easily obscure the fact that throughout the eighteenth century and in large areas of Europe up to 1918, bourgeois people were regarded and treated by the rulers as second-class citizens, people of lower rank.

6 This 'downstairs' world is, of course, the subject of much English comedy and numerous jokes.

17

(few could rival the old-style English butler in knowledge of the gentleman's canon, unless it was the porter of an international hotel). That was not, as far as we can see, the case in Habsburg Austria. The canon of behaviour normal among the acquaintances of Mozart's parents differed far more sharply, as will be seen in more detail later, from the aristocratic court standard.

Leopold Mozart, the servant of princes and court bourgeois, not only educated the young Wolfgang musically in terms of the court taste, but strove to make his behaviour and feelings conform to the court canon as well. As far as the musical tradition was concerned, he succeeded fairly well. As regards behaviour and feelings, his attempt to make Mozart a man of the world failed dismally. He tried to teach him the art of court diplomacy, the currying of favour by adroit circumlocutions, and achieved the opposite. Wolfgang Mozart remained utterly straightforward in his behaviour; just as he showed an immense spontaneity of feeling in his music, he was extraordinarily blunt in his personal conduct. He found it difficult to hide what he felt, or to hint at it indirectly, and hated a form of human intercourse that forced him to use circumlocutions and euphemisms, to beat about the bush. Although he grew up on the fringe of a small court and later travelled from one court to another, he never acquired the special court polish; he never became a man of the world, an *homme du monde*, a gentleman in the eighteenth-century sense. Despite his father's endeavours he retained throughout his life the make-up of a thoroughly middle-class bourgeois.

His attitude was not without inner fissures. He was not unaware of the superiority the court polish conferred on a person, and cannot have been free of the desire to prove himself a gentleman, an *honnête homme*, a man of honour. He refers not infrequently to his 'honour' – this central concept of the aristocratic canon had been absorbed into Mozart's self-image. True, he did not use it in quite the sense of the court model; he meant it to express his claim to equality with court people. And as he had something of the actor in him, he naturally tried to act the courtier. He learned from an early age to dress in the court manner, including the wig, and doubtless also learned the correct way to walk and turn a compliment. But one can imagine that the rascal in him soon began to make fun of court airs and affectations.

A good deal has been written on the role of Mozart's animosity towards the court nobility in his works. But nothing reliable can be said about this unless one investigates how Mozart saw himself in relation to the ruling class of his time.

His situation was a very peculiar one. Although he was the socially dependent subordinate of court aristocrats, his awareness of his extraordinary musical talent made him feel equal, if not superior to them. He was, in a word, a 'genius', an exceptionally gifted creative human being, born into a society which did not yet know the Romantic concept of genius, and whose social canon had no legitimate place for the highly individualised artist of genius in their midst. What, one wonders now, could this have meant for Mozart and his development in human terms? Of course, we can only guess; the evidence is lacking (though not entirely). But just by keeping this strange and in some ways unique situation in mind, we can gain a vital key to understanding Mozart. Without such a reconstruction, without a sense of the structure of his social situation – a genius before the age of genius – our access to him is blocked.

Mozart's own reaction to this situation was many-layered. Black-and-white concepts such as 'friendship' or 'enmity' are quite inadequate to the conflicts and tensions that concern us here. Mozart experienced the fundamental ambivalence of the bourgeois artist in court society, which can be summed up by the following dichotomy: identification with the court nobility and its taste; resentment of his humiliation by it.

Let us begin with the most obvious aspect: his increasing animosity towards court aristocrats who treated him as an inferior. This may have been long in gestation. The prodigy of relatively humble origins will not have been wholly spared the condescending treatment, the humiliation of the bourgeois, that came naturally to most court nobles of the time as part of their social repertoire.

Mozart's disgust with the cavalier treatment meted out to him by court nobles is expressed quite openly in the letters from his Paris period. He has to visit them and do his utmost to earn their favour; for he is looking for a job and needs their recommendation. If he fails to find a position on this journey he will have to go back to Salzburg, to his family, to his father, who has mainly paid for the journey, possibly back to the prince-bishop who can dictate the kind of music he must write and perform. Conditions in Salzburg are like a prison to him. So he waits in Paris on high ladies and gentlemen, who treat him as what he actually is, a servant – if not quite with the tone they use for their coachmen. After all, he writes good music. But he, Mozart, knows that most, though not all, of those whose favour he seeks have only the faintest notion of his music and none at all of his exceptional talent. We must suppose that he became aware of this talent at the time of his successes as a prodigy. His consciousness of the extraordinary nature of his musical imagination may have formed gradually, with many doubts. And now he, who in his own eyes probably never ceased being a prodigy, has to go from one court to another begging for a post. It is fairly certain that he has not foreseen this. His letters reflect a little of his disappointment – and his vexation.

From Paris onwards he seems to have had the impression more and more strongly that it was not just this or that court aristocrat who irritated and humiliated him but that the whole social world in which he lived was somehow wrong. This should not be misunderstood. As far as we can tell, Mozart was not interested in general, rather abstract human-itarian or political ideals. His social protest was expressed at most in comments such as: 'You know well that the best and truest of all friends are the poor. The wealthy do not know

what friendship means'.[7] He found the treatment he received unjust, was angered by it and fought against it in his
way. But it was always a very personal fight. This was not
the least reason why he had to lose.

Added to this, as we have said, was Mozart's lack of the
relaxed elegance, the wit, the dexterity in verbal skirmishes
needed in court circles to steer one's ship past the hidden
reefs and abysses to the desired goal. It is difficult to decide
whether he was unwilling or unable to assimilate the court
canon of feeling and behaviour which was at least as
important to the success of his search for a post as musical
qualifications. Perhaps the two things, unwillingness and
inability, went together. Be that as it may, we find in him the
symptoms of a conflict of canons that was fought out at least
as much within himself as between him and other people.
Mozart liked to dress elegantly in the court manner. But for
those arts that would have won people over to him in these
circles, and on which largely depended their support for his
applications, he had no special aptitude. And he lacked
almost entirely that specific knowledge of people that
enabled courtiers instantaneously to identify those who
belonged by their criteria and those who did not, and to
adjust their behaviour towards them accordingly.

Mozart seeking a job in Paris is the kind of episode one
does not easily forget. He was angered and wounded by his
treatment, and really had no idea what was going on.
Mozart's one-man revolution, his attempt to break out of the
predicament in which he depended on an aristocratic
superior who also controlled his music, was beginning
slowly to take shape.

---

7 Cf. Hildesheimer, *op. cit.*, p. 89. The quotation comes from a letter of 7 August
1778: *The Letters of Mozart and his Family* (chronologically arranged, translated
and edited by Emily Anderson, London 1985, p. 593. (Referred to from here on
as *LMF*; quotations from letters are taken from this source. References to Mozart's
correspondence without quotations are from: *Mozart, Briefe und Aufzeichnungen*,
complete edition, collected and annotated by Wilhelm A. Bauer and Otto Erich
Deutsch [and Joseph Heinz Eibl], 7 vols, Kassel/Basle/London/New York
1962–75.) Only the volume and page numbers are given in the notes.

However, this layer of his personal revolt was clearly linked indissolubly with another, his revolt against his father. Leopold Mozart had trained his son for a career as a musician in court society. We must keep in mind how closely, looked at sociologically, his behaviour was linked to the old craftsman tradition.[8] Within this framework it was commonplace for a father to take on the role of the master instructing his son in the craft skills, perhaps even hoping that his son would one day surpass his own mastery. We certainly get a more complete and well-rounded picture of the peculiarity of the musical tradition of the seventeenth and eighteenth centuries – at court and in the church – if we bear in mind that music still had much of the character of a craft, and that especially in the court sphere it was marked by a very sharp social inequality between the art producer and the patron.

Leopold Mozart was still fairly firmly rooted in this tradition. He brought up his son in line with its canon. A social position as a court musician was a part of it. The total failure of his son's expensive quest for a post in places such as Paris was a bitter disappointment to him. He managed to persuade the prince-bishop of Salzburg to take back the failed escapee as leader of the orchestra and court organist in recognition of his brilliant gifts. At the beginning of 1779, therefore, Wolfgang Mozart was back in his native town, under the direct supervision of his father and the rule of his old master, who was also the master of Leopold Mozart. In this second Salzburg phase Mozart wrote what was to be for the time being the last of his operas in the traditional court style, *Idomeneo*, an opera seria, the libretto of which, in keeping with the canon of the obsolute court, fittingly praised a prince for his kindness and generosity.

In 1781, a few months after the first performance of *Idomeneo*, Mozart broke with the prince-bishop; with utmost difficulty he obtained his release by the expedient of the

8   This tradition explains why families of artists like the Mozarts, or the Bachs, are found again and again in Germany.

famous kick 'in the behind'. This was the climax of his personal revolt against the imposition of a subordinate role as servant to an absolute ruler.

Mozart's father was still more or less solidly a court bourgeois. As a social construction, a princely court had a strictly hierarchical form, that of a steep pyramid. Leopold Mozart fitted into this structure, perhaps not without troubles, not without the vulnerability of the outsider. But the compulsion of the figuration was, for him, inescapable. He knew his place, devoted himself to it body and soul, and expected the same of his son. He expected great things of Wolfgang – at a court, preferably a bigger one than Salzburg, perhaps the Bavarian court in Munich, or even Paris; such were the father's ambitions. His son did not fulfil them. His failure at the German courts or with the patricians of Augsburg was not, in the end, irremediable. But then Wolfgang Mozart gave notice to his Salzburg employer. From his father's point of view this step was incomprehensible. As he must have seen it his son was gravely damaging his career, his prospects as a court musician. What was he to live on?

As we can see, the son's revolt was directed equally at his father, the court bourgeois, and at the archbishop, the ruling court aristocrat.

Again with the presumption of people living in a later age, one can say retrospectively that, within the existing structure of Austrian society in general and the music profession in particular, Mozart's personal revolt had little chance of achieving its desired end. But what we would have lost if he had not undertaken it! For it is hardly conceivable that this break by one of the best-known figures in the musical world of his time with the usual conditions of service, the socially prescribed scheme of his profession, did not affect his work as a composer.

It is useful to view Mozart's skirmish with the archbishop of Salzburg from a somewhat greater distance, in a wider context. Through this conflict in the microcosm of the

Salzburg court we shall then see, represented as it were through two individuals, the wider conflicts in the macrocosm of the society of the time. We see that in the widest sense they involved a conflict between a ruling prince, a member of the high nobility who was also a high church dignitary, and a member of the petty bourgeoisie, whose father had worked his way up from craftsman status to that of a court servant.

However, the ready-made formula about the bourgeoisie rising as a result of an inner necessity of social development in the second half of the eighteenth century, defeating a feudal nobility undermined by economic change in the French Revolution, tends to be applied in such a routine, mechanical way today that one loses sight of the complex course of actual events. The observable problems of human beings are categorised by class concepts debased to clichés, such as 'nobility' and 'bourgeoisie', 'feudalism' and 'capitalism'. Categories like these block access to a better understanding of the development of music and of art in general. Such understanding is only possible if the discussion is not restricted either to economic processes or to developments in music, and if an attempt is made at the same time to illuminate the changing fate of the people who produce music and other works of art within the developing structure of society.

It is quite clear that in Mozart's youth the ascendancy of the absolutist princes and the court aristocracy (who are sometimes lumped together with the nobility at a different stage of social development, the feudal nobility of the Middle Ages) was still completely intact. Relatively untouched by the French Revolution, it continued to exist throughout his life in the Habsburg empire as in many German and Italian regions. There and elsewhere a court establishment clung to its position as the highest-ranking social group, with slowly waning dominance, till late in the nineteenth century and in some cases, as in the great European empires, until the 1914–18 war. To be sure, the power relationships of the European states changed during that period, as did the social position of artists and the character of the arts. But structural changes in the arts in the early and mid nineteenth century can scarcely be understood if they are merely characterised as 'bourgeois' and the influence of the aristocratic courts is forgotten.

Mozart's conflict with his aristocratic employer, and indeed the whole course of his life, thus show paradigmatically how dependent a bourgeois musician was at that time – unlike a bourgeois writer – on a position at a court, or at least within a court patriciate. All the same, there was in Germany (with Austria) and in Italy one possibility of escape for musicians, a chance to seek different employment if one was dissatisfied with what one had. This opportunity was bound up with the peculiar structure of rule in these territories (and not with the rise of the bourgeoisie). It was of utmost importance for the development of music in the German and Italian regions.

The failed attempts at integration north and south of the Alps by the imperial as well as the papist central rulers of the territories which followed the Holy Roman Empire gave rise to a number of smaller states at a lower level of integration. In the countries that had centralised earlier, especially France and England, there has existed from the seventeenth century a single court that surpassed all other noble households in power, wealth and cultural influence. Germany and Italy, by contrast, were fragmented into an almost incalculable number of court establishments, or urban ones orientated towards courts. To give one example: in Mozart's time the fairly small area of present-day Swabia was split into 96 different dominions – 4 church princes, 14 secular princes, 25 landlords, 30 imperial cities and 23 prelates.[9] In a good number of these sovereign territories absolute rulers maintained an official organisation which included an orchestra of employed musicians as an item essential for prestige. This multiplicity was the distinctive feature of the musical landscape in Germany and Italy.

---

9 Arthur Hutchings, *Mozart – der Mensch*, Baarn 1976, p. 11.

In France and England the decisive musical positions were concentrated in the capitals, Paris and London, as a result of state centralisation. A high-ranking musician in these countries therefore had no chance of escape if he fell out with his princely employer. There were no competing courts that could rival the king's in power, wealth and prestige, and that could have given refuge to, for example, a French musician who had fallen from favour. But in Germany and Italy there were dozens of courts and cities competing for prestige, and thus for musicians. It is no exaggeration to trace the extraordinary productivity of court music in the territories of the former German empire among other things to this figuration – to the rivalry for prestige of the many courts and the correspondingly high number of musical posts.[10]

This figuration was the precondition for the relatively large number of professional musicians working in Italy and Germany at that time. It was also a factor that strengthened the musicians' hand in their dealings with their employers. If an artist employed at the French court resigned his post, the only possibility open to him was to earn a living at a non-French court, which in the eyes of most French artists was much the same as demotion. It was different in Italy and Germany. There we hear again and again of artist craftsmen who had a disagreement with their princely master and removed themselves in one way or another to a different territory. When Michelangelo came into conflict with the pope he set off for Florence and retorted to the papal bailiffs sent to fetch him back that he would not return. When Bach fell out with his employer, the duke of Weimar, he resigned his post, having already used his contacts to line up a

---

10 The comparison with England, where little outstanding music was produced in the eighteenth century, apart from imports, suggests that the greater musical productivity in the states of the former Holy Roman Empire may also have been connected to another structural peculiarity, the different relationship between nobility and bourgeoisie existing in the two areas. In Germany the barriers between the two classes were relatively high, with few crossing points. The social and political subordination of bourgeois people to the nobility, especially the court nobility, was much stricter and more pronounced than in England.

position at another court. The furious duke had him locked up in prison for his insubordination, but he resisted stubbornly and finally obtained his release.

In this latter episode the resemblance to Mozart's case is striking. But such incidents are not important merely for biographers or for the fate of the individual musician concerned. They are seen in the proper light only if they are understood as being characteristic of the structure and power differences in court society.

Mozart Becomes a Freelance Artist

What Mozart's decision to give up service in Salzburg really meant was this: instead of being the permanent employee of a patron he wanted to earn his living henceforth as a 'freelance artist', by selling his skill as a musician and his works on the open market.

For literary products a kind of free market existed in Germany in the eighteenth century, in connection with the proliferation of petty states. There were early forms of a publishing industry, that is, more or less specialised commercial ventures concerned with the printing, distribution and sale of literary works. An educated bourgeois public interested in German books – often in deliberate contrast to a court nobility primarily interested in French writing at that time – was gaining size. In this way the social figure of the 'freelance writer' emerged in the eighteenth century – though only tentatively, since it was still very difficult, as far as we can see, for a person to support himself and his family on the income from books sold on the market, without the help of a noble patron. Lessing's life is an example of this. All the same, the free market existed. There was a public of educated bourgeois scattered right across Germany who had enough income to buy books and were willing to do so. The character and form of the German literary movement in the second half of the eighteenth century reflected this social figuration.

In the sphere of music this development was relatively retarded. Mozart's decision to set himself up as a freelance artist came at a time when the social structure actually offered no such place for outstanding musicians. The emergence of a music market and the corresponding institutions was only just beginning. The organisation of concerts for a paying public, and the activities of publishers who sold works by well-known composers and paid them fees in advance, were, at most, in the very early stages. In particular, the institutions needed for a market extending beyond the local level were largely lacking.[1] In Austria and most German territories the great majority of concerts and, above all, operas, which were Mozart's primary interest as a composer, were arranged and financed for an invited public by court aristocrats (or urban patricians).[2] It is doubtful whether another highly qualified musician could be found at that time who had tried in the same way to make himself independent of court patronage and the secure position of a court servant.

Whether he knew it or not, therefore, Mozart was taking an extraordinary risk when he broke with his patron. He was putting his life, his whole social existence, at stake.

His ideas about what the future was to bring were probably not very precise. The situation in Salzburg had become unbearable – the negative side was quite clear to him, and to understand his person and his situation it is not unimportant to imagine how Mozart felt. His employer

1 Mozart did not produce the piano arrangement of *Die Entführung aus dem Serail* quickly enough – two publishers rushed it on to the market without paying him a penny. There was no legal protection. For each of his operas he probably received only a single fee, though he would have been paid something more if he conducted it.

2 The development of the musical concert clearly happened in three stages: concerts for an invited audience, then by subscription and finally for an unknown paying public. At Mozart's time the last stage had not been reached, at least in Vienna. He had to bear the risk for his concerts himself – hence the need for advance payment, a subscription showing that enough people were interested to prevent the event making a loss.

prescribed when and where he was to give a concert, and often enough what he should compose. That was nothing unusual. It probably did not go beyond the terms of a normal contract of employment. In keeping with the conditions of their craft all professional musicians with permanent positions had lived, exactly like goldsmiths or painters, under the constraints that Mozart no longer tolerated. Some of them, like Couperin or Johann Sebastian Bach, had produced great works. It may be that Mozart had fallen foul of a particularly obdurate employer, but that is not the point here. What is decisive is that, in his personal goals and wishes, in his sense of what had meaning and what did not, he anticipated the attitudes and feelings of a later type of artist. Institutionally, the court situation of the official, salaried artist still prevailed at his time. But in his personality structure he was someone who wanted above all to follow his own imagination. In other words, Mozart represented the free artist who places his trust largely in individual inspiration, at a time when the performance and composition of the music valued highest by society was still as good as exclusively in the hands of craft musicians with permanent posts either at courts or with the urban churches. The social distribution of power that was expressed in this form of music production was by and large intact.

For all his recklessness, Mozart did have certain ideas about his future. His hopes were pinned on what is perhaps best described as good Viennese society. Its most influential groups were families from the court nobility, among whom he had acquaintances and friends. To begin with he wanted to try to earn his living by giving music lessons and concerts, for which high-placed ladies and gentlemen would invite him to their houses or that were arranged for him. He intended to hold 'academies' – concerts the income from which went directly into the pockets of the performers – and he hoped to raise subscriptions for the printed scores of his compositions. He was, as he knew, very popular in Viennese society. Some members of these circles had already promised him their support. In addition, he had a considerable reputation outside Vienna. But there can be little doubt that he had set his heart entirely on success in the Austrian capital.

For some years this success actually materialised. On 3 March 1784 Mozart wrote to his father that he was shortly, on the last three Wednesdays of Lent, to hold three subscription concerts, for which he already had a hundred subscribers and might get thirty more. He was also planning two academies – for all of which he needed 'new things'. In the mornings he was giving piano lessons and almost every evening he played in noble houses.[3] His subscribers – we have some of the lists – were also nobles. But on 12 July 1789 he mentions to the merchant Michael Puchberg that a new concert subscription of his has failed because he had only one name on the list: Herr van Swieten, a close acquaintance of his.[4] Viennese society had turned away from him, with the emperor at its head.[5]

We can recognise here the peculiarity of the market that Mozart had at his disposal. Even as a 'freelance artist' he was really still dependent, like every craft artist, on a limited local circle of clients. This was a fairly closed, tightly integrated circle. If word went round in it that the emperor did not think especially highly of a musician, good society simply dropped him.[6]

In considering Mozart's existence as a 'freelance artist' we again encounter the deep-rooted ambivalence that was

---

3 III, pp. 303f.
4 IV, p. 92.
5 The turning point was probably *The Marriage of Figaro*, the subject of which – chosen by Mozart himself – was regarded as politically suspect from the absolutist standpoint. A noble noted in his diary at the time that he had seen the opera and had *sich ennuyiert* (Hildesheimer, *op. cit.*, p. 199). That does not mean, as it is sometimes translated, that he was 'bored', but 'annoyed'.
6 Perhaps the defeat that Mozart suffered through these events, the sense of lost meaning, was all the harder to bear because he was one of the first composers of the modern period, if not the first, whose imagination had run far ahead of his listeners' habits. The fate of the artist deserted by his public could not yet be seen as a recurrent phenomenon. Mozart must undoubtedly have perceived it as something that affected him alone.

characteristic of his attitude towards the court aristocracy and that was to determine his whole life. It has several facets.

As has been described, Mozart had in any case absorbed the canon of behaviour of the ruling class of his time. At the same time his musical imagination was formed by and steeped in the court-aristocratic tradition of music making. Whereas a man like Beethoven broke out of this tradition, Mozart never did so. He developed his individual possibilities of giving expression to feelings within the framework of the old canons within which he had grown up. And it is precisely because he developed the sequential ordering of the motifs that rose up in him *within* the traditional canon that his music is so accessible and has such lasting appeal.

The highest-ranking musical work on the court society's scale of values was the opera. It was consistent with this social valuation that the composing of operas had for Mozart the emotional value of the highest personal fulfilment. But institutionally an opera, with the immense expense it entailed, was tied almost exclusively to the courts – unlike a play, for example, which could be performed by a travelling company of actors. It was the court aristocracy that saw in opera a fitting form of entertainment. Mozart, who decided to be a 'free' artist, had in part adopted the court musical tradition among his ideals, as a layer of his own person.

The same fixation revealed itself in his personal attitude to his public – even after he had broken with the archbishop. When Mozart was about to take this step, a member of the Salzburg court warned him with almost prophetic foresight that the favour of court society in Vienna was very fickle: 'Here a person's fame does not last long,' said this man, 'after a few months the Viennese want something new.'[7] But Mozart had pinned all his hopes on success with the Viennese public, with public opinion in the high society of the capital. This was clearly one of the highest-ranking

7 See p. 119 below.

wishes of his life – and one of the most important reasons for his tragedy.

I suggested at the outset that one cannot determine from a he-perspective what a person experiences as fulfilling his desires and meanings and what as depriving him of them. One must try to see it from the first-person viewpoint, the I-perspective. It happens far less infrequently than might be expected that someone sets his heart with special fervour on the applause of his immediate circle of friends and acquaintances, the approval and acclaim of the town where he lives, and that success somewhere else in the world cannot outweigh the lack of success, or even the rejection, he experiences in the narrower circle to which he is bound. Something of this constellation is to be found in the life of Mozart.

If we follow this thread, we also find that Mozart's attitude and situation cannot in fact be properly understood if his attitude to court society is seen as purely negative – a rejection of the kind commonly found in the German bourgeois literature of the second half of the eighteenth century.[8] His personal rebellion against the humiliation and constraint he suffered in court circles, whether in seeking employment or as an employee, has at first sight something in common with the revolt, mainly in non-Austrian parts of the German empire, which found expression in the humanitarian literature whose guiding concepts were education (*Bildung*) and culture (*Kultur*). Like the bourgeois

8 It is not without interest to point out this difference. For one of the most astonishing peculiarities of the 1770s and 1780s in Germany is the fact that the two worlds in which Mozart lived, the court-bourgeois and the court-aristocratic worlds, were, as far as one can tell, practically untouched by the great wave of the German literary and philosophical movement going on at the same time. In the 1770s, when many young Germans were giving themselves up to the excitement of the *Sturm und Drang* – Goethe's *Götz* came out in 1773, Klinger's *Sturm und Drang* in 1774, Lenz's *Der Hofmeister* in 1776, *Die Soldaten* in 1778 – the young Mozart found success, especially in Italy but then in Germany as well, with operas in the traditional seria style. In 1778, the year Kant's *Critique of Pure Reason* was published, *Idomeneo*, written to a commission from the Bavarian court, was given its first performance in Munich. It is one of Mozart's finest and most inventive operas, conforming entirely to court taste yet unique in its development of the old tradition.

forerunners of this philosophical and literary movement, Mozart insisted on the human dignity that was his regardless of his social origin or rank. Unlike his father, he never accepted in his innermost self his position as a lower-ranking person. He never reconciled himself to the fact that he and his music were treated with condescension.

But in Mozart's case the resentment and bitterness he felt towards aristocrats who conveyed to him that ultimately he was only a subordinate, a kind of higher entertainer, took its justification only marginally from general principles. He did not call on an ideology of universal humanity to support it. His lack of interest in such ideals was another factor distinguishing him from Beethoven, not merely on the individual plane but on that of generations. His feeling of equality, and his demand that he be treated as an equal, appear, as far as we can see, to have been founded primarily on his music – his work and his achievement. He was aware of his music's high value, and therefore his own, from an early age. His negative feelings and his rebellion against aristocrats who treated him contemptuously were only one side of the coin. We cannot properly understand Mozart's life or his work unless we realise how ambiguous his attitude to court society was.

Up to a point he had the same conflicting feelings towards his father. But here his urge to break free gained the upper hand fairly clearly – despite his protestations of obedience and devotion. Mozart's behaviour seems to indicate that the negative components of his feelings towards his father became gradually more exacerbated, although his conscience never quite allowed him to abandon the posture of the devoted son.

In Mozart's relationship to the ruling class, with whose members he had to deal as a person of bourgeois, i.e. lower origin, the positive side of his ambivalent feelings probably remained stronger than *vis-à-vis* his father. In the context of an established–outsider relationship[9] – and we are dealing

---

9 On the theory of such relationships cf. Norbert Elias and John L. Scotson, *Etablierte und Aussenseiter*, Frankfurt am Main 1990.

with such a relationship here – that is not unusual; in this respect, too, the individual case has a certain paradigmatic significance.

Like many people in an outsider position, Mozart suffered under the humiliations inflicted on him by court nobles, and was angered by them. But hand in hand with such hostile reactions to the higher class went strong positive feelings: it was precisely their recognition he sought, precisely by them that he wanted to be regarded and treated as a man of equal worth, on account of his musical achievements. This ambivalence was expressed, for example, in his energetic rebuff to his court employer, and his simultaneous desire to win the favour of the predominantly court-aristocratic Viennese public as a 'freelance artist'.

The kind of feelings and the attitude we encounter here are an example of a figuration that is not infrequently observed in connection with a certain type of outsider-establishment relationship. People who hold the position of outsiders in relation to certain established groups, but who feel equal or even superior to them on grounds of their personal achievements or sometimes even their wealth, may bitterly resist the humiliations to which they are exposed; they may also be fully aware of the human frailties of the established group. But as long as the power of the establishment remains intact it and its canon of behaviour and feeling can exert a strong attraction on outsiders. It is often the latters' greatest wish to be recognised as equals by those who treat them so openly as their inferiors. The curious fixation of the wishes of people in outsider positions on recognition and acceptance by their establishment causes this goal to become the focus of all their acts and desires, their source of meaning. No other esteem, no other success carries so much weight for them as the esteem of the one circle in which they are regarded as inferior outsiders, as success in their local establishment. Precisely that success was finally denied Mozart.

Because the success of his music in Vienna had special importance for him, his later failure there affected him all the more deeply. In the last years of his life he had considerable success in other cities of the German empire, but it seems that this could not outweigh his gradual loss of popularity in Vienna. Understanding of his music in Viennese society clearly gave special meaning to his life, just as the incomprehension of the same circles and the breaking-off of many personal contacts (to which he doubt-less contributed) meant an equally heavy loss of meaning. This experience played a decisive part in the feeling of meaninglessness and despair that seems to have overtaken him at the end of his life, that bitterly distressed him and finally deprived him of the courage to struggle on and fight the illness that attacked him.

The fact that Mozart gave up his relatively secure post at the small court of the prince-bishop of Salzburg to earn his living in Vienna certainly did not mean that he planned at that stage to build himself a position as a 'freelance artist', even in the limited sense in which Beethoven and other famous musicians of the nineteenth century were able to do so. Creative musicians who want to publish their works and earn money with them are always more dependent on the collaboration of other people than exponents of arts such as poetry or painting. If they are not themselves able to function as concert organisers, conductors, opera directors, etc., they need other people to fill these roles if their compositions are to be made available to a wider public. We need to consider this need for co-operation, too, with all the tensions and chances for conflict it contained, if we are to gauge the prospects of professional success and income that Mozart had when he resigned his post as a permanent court employee.

The development of the market for high-quality music has, by and large, the same structure and direction, the same sequential order, as markets of other kinds. Today there is an international market for Mozart's musical creations, but also for some works by contemporary composers who have gained access to the concert halls in the capitals of the world, and to broadcasts on the media, in a hard competitive struggle. The potential market awaiting Mozart as he exchanged the career of a court musician for that of a relatively freelance artist was, as we have said, much narrower. Institutions that were capable of mounting operas, ballets and large-scale orchestral works were still largely confined to cities with courts, such as Munich, Mannheim, Berlin or Prague. At Mozart's time Vienna, the seat of the imperial court, held a very high position among them, while the cultural movements, principally in literature and philosophy, flourishing in other German regions, which addressed a bourgeois public outside the courts, were somewhat stunted in Vienna. As an audience for the elite music of the time, the kind that Mozart wrote, the aristocratic court society still played the leading role.

By giving up the court service that he detested Mozart did not become independent of the court audience. On the contrary, it was, above all, members of Viennese aristocratic society, such as prince Gallitzin or the Thun family, who had awakened in him the idea that he could earn an independent living on the local music market, without an employer or a secure income. It may be that he was also counting on commissions from the imperial family, which, within limits, he later actually received. Or he may have been hoping for a position at the imperial court – which, within limits, he also achieved. For he was certainly not opposed to permanent posts in principle, and in fact spent his life looking for one. Mozart did not get into the position of a 'freelance artist' simply because that was his desired goal; he did so because he could not stand his work at the Salzburg court any longer.

On the other hand, the vision of the famous, independent artist travelling between countries from court to court had also beguiled his father for a time. Since Mozart had already tasted the life free of a permanent employer, with its toil and its joys, as a child, when he moved from one 'good society' to another, it would be surprising if this possibility had not remained in his mind as a more fulfilling alternative to service at court. The decisive influence this period had on Mozart's character is quite evident. Over and over again he strove for the glow of admiring acceptance that he had known for a time as a child.

And he knew very well that he deserved it just as much in his later life. He never had a low opinion of himself or his work, and seldom relaxed in his labour for his art. His early training had helped him acquire the ability to improvise musically in the taste of his time, that is, in the manner required by the canon of the ruling class. That an artist had to follow the taste of his socially superior audience was, as far as music was concerned, still taken for granted. The power structure that gave the court nobility precedence before all other classes also determined what kind of music a bourgeois artist could make in court circles and how far he could go with innovations. Even as a 'freelance artist' Mozart was bound to this structure.

Mozart always dreamed of being able to create freely, to follow his inner voices without worrying about a buyer.[10] Even in Salzburg he had written his best pieces for someone whom he wanted to oblige, where he could give his imagination free rein. He believed he would have this possibility in Vienna. But there too he was forced to compromise. Let us take as an example some piano concertos he composed in the mid-1780s. It was a vital necessity for him to satisfy public taste with these works, as he depended on the income from his 'academies'.

On 11 December 1784 he completed a concerto in F major (K 459), with drums and trumpets playing *tutti*, which he performed six years later at the coronation of Emperor Leopold II in Frankfurt. This was a work written with the public uppermost in mind, with bravado and

---

10 His sublimation-patterns were peculiar. When he composed an opera, and was constrained only by the libretto (which he always chose with great care to match his needs), the text clearly released the fetters on his imagination. His music flowed spontaneously, heightening the words with its magic. It was not quite the same with other kinds of music.

---

ostentatious virtuosity. But as if disgusted by this subordination of his creative powers to a higher force, as if he were rebelling, two months later he wrote an entirely different piano concerto, the one in D minor (K 466). In part it is a work of dramatic, passionate intensity. One has the feeling that he is entirely indifferent to what people might think. He is writing music as he feels it, perhaps even with the conscious or unconscious intention to shock — *pour épater la noblesse*. He did not make himself more popular by this, and he needed money. Incidentally, this was his only concerto that was well known in the nineteenth century. But Mozart did not continue in this direction for the time being. In the winter and spring of 1785/6 he wrote three new concertos, of which Alfred Einstein writes in his perceptive book: 'The first two [in E flat, K 482 and in A, K 488] give us the impression that he felt he had perhaps gone too far, had given the Viennese public credit for too much, had overstepped the boundaries of "social" music – or, more simply stated, that he saw the favour of the public waning, and sought to win it back with works that would be sure of success.'[11]

In 1789 Mozart went to Berlin, where the cello-playing king commissioned six string quartets and six easy sonatas for his daughter, who played the piano. So he had commissions. But one can see Mozart becoming aware that, for this patron, he would have to simplify what he heard, so that it no longer interested him. He did not want to simplify. He wanted to follow his inner voices and write *them* down. So he finished only three of the quartets for the Brandenburg court, and only one of the piano sonatas. The need to write for himself, a general characteristic of musicians today, was asserting itself more and more.

Beethoven was born in 1770, almost fifteen years after Mozart. He achieved, not easily, but with far less trouble, what Mozart fruitlessly strove for: he liberated himself

---

11 Alfred Einstein, *Mozart – his Character, his Work* (trans. by a. Mendel and N. Broder), London/Toronto/Melbourne/Sydney 1946, p. 309.

largely from the dependence on court patronage. He was thus able to follow his own voice in his compositions – or more exactly, the immanent sequential order of his inner voices, rather than the conventional taste of his customers. Beethoven had a far greater opportunity to impose his taste on the musical public. Unlike Mozart, he was able to escape the compulsion to produce music as a subordinate for a far more powerful employer or patron; instead, he could compose music, if not exclusively then to a far greater extent, as a freelance artist (as we call it today) for a relatively unknown public. A short quotation may be enough to illustrate the difference. In June 1801 Beethoven wrote to his friend Wegeler: 'My compositions bring me in a good deal; and I may say that I am offered more commissions than it is possible for me to carry out. Moreover, for every composition I can count on six or seven publishers, and even more, if I want them; people no longer come to an arrangement with me, I state my price and they pay. So you can see how pleasantly situated I am.'[12]

Mozart had dreamed of attaining what Beethoven triumphantly announces here as having been attained; and who knows, perhaps he too would have achieved it if he had had the courage to live longer. In line with current modes of thought one might be tempted to think that by the same age of thirty-one Mozart, like Beethoven, could have got himself into a position where publishers competed for his work, if he had adapted himself more to the taste of the wider public. But one should not give way too quickly to the conventional pressure that inclines us to explain such differences in the careers of two people primarily by individual differences, and to dismiss explanations based on structural changes in society. After his death, Mozart was not short of success. What he lacked in his lifetime was the more developed music publishing activity that Beethoven indicates in his letter (and the spread of concerts given for a paying rather

---

12 *The Letters of Beethoven.* collected, edited and translated by Emily Anderson, vol. I, London 1961, p. 58.

than an invited audience). Indeed, there are few statements which highlight a deep structural change in the social position of artists more vividly than this: 'people no longer come to an arrangement with me, I state my price and they pay.'

Moreover, the change hinted at in this statement does not concern merely the social position of the artist. With it, the canon of artistic creation or, expressed differently, the structure of art, also changed. But such connections do not emerge very clearly if the transition from art production for a personally known employer or patron to art production for a paying public, from patronage to the free, more or less anonymous market, is considered merely as an economic event. To take this view is to overlook an essential point: that this was a structural change in the relation of people to each other, which can be precisely defined. In particular, it involved a power-gain by the artist in relation to his public. This human change, this change in the balance of power – not simply between individuals as such but between them as representatives of different social functions and positions, between people in their capacity as artists and as public – remains incomprehensible as long as the pattern of our thinking aims solely at spinning out dehumanised abstractions. We can do it justice only if we have clear examples before our eyes and if we try to visualise what this change meant for the people concerned.

Craftsmen's Art and Artists' Art

In deciding to quit his service in Salzburg and entrust his future to the favour of Viennese good society without a permanent post, Mozart was taking a very unusual step for a musician of his rank at that time. But it was of the utmost importance for his musical production. For the canon of music production by court artists who worked for a particular employer, according to his instructions and needs, differed strikingly, on account of the specific social figuration in which their music had its function, from the new canon which gradually formed as music production by relatively free artists competing for a mainly anonymous public became the rule. To express this in traditional terms: with the changed social position and function of music makers, the style and character of their music also changed. The special quality of Mozart's music undoubtedly stems from the uniqueness of his gift. But the way this gift expressed itself in his works is very closely bound up with the fact that he, a court musician, took the step to 'freelance' status in a sense too early, at a time when social development allowed such a step but was not quite ready for it institutionally.

However, the difficulty and recklessness of this step emerge clearly only if it is seen in the wider context of the development leading from craftsmen's art to artists' art, from art production for particular patrons, usually social superiors, to production for the anonymous market, for a public which is by and large the artist's equal. Mozart's social existence, the peculiarity of his social fate, shows very clearly that the switch from craftsmen's art to 'free' artistic creation was not an abrupt event. What took place in reality was a process with many intermediate stages, the central phase of transformation occurring later in the case of music, as can be seen, than in the case of literature and painting. Mozart's life is easier to understand if is it seen as a micro-process within the central transformation period of this macro-process.

To point out that what is usually called the 'history' of art is not just a kaleidoscopic sequence of change, an unstructured succession of styles or even a fortuitous accumulation of 'great' men, but a definite, ordered sequence, a structured process going in a certain direction and closely bound up with the overall social process, is not to imply a hidden heteronomous valuation. It is not to suggest that the art of 'free' artists for a market of unknown customers is better or worse than that of craftsmen produced for patrons. From the standpoint of our present-day feelings the change in the artist's position under discussion here may well have been a change 'for the better' for the people concerned. But that does not mean it was such for their works. In the course of the changing relationship between those who produce art and those who need and buy it, the structure of art changes, not its value.[1]

As Mozart's revolt in the sphere of music represented a step forward in the transition from the employed to the 'free' artist, it is worthwhile to consider one or two aspects of the change in the position of the artist and the structure of art

---

1 To be sure, we often find that posterity values highest the works an artist-craftsman has produced from pure joy or under the pressure of acute suffering, without thinking about public taste or financial gain. For example, the paintings by Vermeer of Delft that are now regarded as his most important were unsold and no doubt unsaleable works left behind after his death.

that this unplanned process brought with it. This can be done best if the artist and his customers are imagined standing on the two pans of a scale, like weights. This implies that the relationship between artists and consumers, no matter how many intermediate links there may be between them, involves a specific power balance. With the transition from craftsmen's art to artists' art this balance changes.

In the phase of craftsmen's art the patrons' canon of taste as a framework for artistic creation had preponderance over the personal fantasy of every artist. Individual imagination was channelled strictly according to the taste of the established patron class. In the phase of artists' art those creating art are in general socially equal to the public which enjoys and buys art. In the case of their leading cadres, their specialist establishment in a given country, artists as the moulders of taste and the vanguard of art are more powerful than their public. With their innovative models they can lead the established canon of art in new directions, and the broad public may then slowly learn to see with their eyes and hear with their ears.

The direction taken by this change in the relationship between art producers and art consumers and *pari passu* in the structure of art certainly does not exist in isolation. It is one strand in the wider development of the social units which provide the framework of reference for artistic creation at a given time. And it can be observed only where the development of the social framework is moving in the corresponding direction, that is, in conjunction with a growing differentiation and individualisation of many other social functions, or with the displacement of the court aristocracy by a professional bourgeois public as the upper class, and thus as the recipients and consumers of works of art. On the other hand, such a change in the relation of art producers to art consumers is by no means strictly tied to the particular sequence of events in Europe. A change in a similar direction is found, for example, in the alteration in the craftsmen's art of African tribes as they reach a higher stage of integration, where the previous tribal units merge into state units. Here too craft production, perhaps of an ancestral figure or a mask, slowly frees itself from dependence on a particular buyer or a particular occasion within a village, and changes into production for a market of anonymous people, such as the tourist market or the international art market mediated by dealers.

Wherever social processes of the kind just sketched take place, specific changes in the canon of art-creation and, correspondingly, in the structural quality of art-works are discernible. These latter changes are always linked to a social change affecting the people bound together as art producers and consumers. Unless the connection between them is clarified the two sets of changes can at best be superficially described, but hardly explained or made comprehensible.

Mozart's fate is a moving illustration of the problems encountered by a person who, as a musician of very unusual talent, became caught up in this unplanned social process. Of course, he also got into his situation through a very personal decision; for it was unquestionably his own choice to give up the employment that offered a modest but fairly secure income to seek his fortune as a freelance artist in Vienna. But his resignation from his court post, although almost unprecedented among musicians, did not happen at random. It is unlikely that Mozart had not, in Paris or the German cities, caught some of the wind of bourgeois protest against the claims to dominance of the privileged court nobility. Whereas Leopold Mozart had finally – if reluctantly – bowed to his own social fate, since no way out of the court-aristocratic order of things was open to a musician of his generation, his son belonged to a generation for which the hope of a way out did not seem quite so vain, or the desire to earn a living on one's own merits as a musician, even without fixed employment, quite so difficult to fulfil. The opportunities for freelance artists had somewhat increased, even though the leap into 'freedom' actually meant little more than a somewhat looser dependence on the court-aristocratic public. And as this public was capricious, it involved no inconsiderable risk.

Of course, it was Mozart's decision to resign his post and risk this leap. But even such individual decisions remain ultimately opaque if we overlook the relevant aspects of the unplanned social processes within which they are taken, the dynamics of which largely determine their consequences. If we can reconstruct what the broad change in the relation of art producers to art recipients meant for the experience and situation of the former, and so for the nature of their works, we can gain a clearer and deeper understanding of an individual artist who took, like Mozart – half pulling, half pulled – a few steps in the direction of this process.

To get a clearer picture of this process we should imagine two positions within it which are polar opposites, two stages very far apart in the structural change undergone by the relationship between the producers and consumers of art. In one case, where a craftsman-artist works for a particular client known to him, the product is usually created for a specific purpose prescribed by society. It might be a public festivity or a private ritual – whatever it is, the creation of an art product requires the personal fantasy of the producer to be subordinated to a social canon of art-making sanctified by tradition and secured by the power of the art recipient. In this case, therefore, the form of the art work is shaped less by its function for the individual producer and more by its function for the client and user, in keeping with the structure of the power-ratio.

Here, the art users do not comprise an accumulation of individual art consumers, each of whom is relatively highly individualised, embodying in isolation from the others the instrument, as it were, with which the art-work resonates. Rather, art is attuned to recipients who, even independently of the occasion on which art works are presented, form a fairly tightly knit group. The art-work derives its place and function for the group from fixed occasions when they come together – for example, at an opera performance. Not the least of the art-work's functions, therefore, is as a means for the society to display itself, both as a group and as individuals within a group. The decisive instrument with which the work resonates is not so much individuals in themselves – each alone with his or her feelings – but many individual people integrated into a group, people whose feelings are largely mobilised by and orientated towards their being together. At these earlier stages the social occasions for which art-works were produced were not, as in our day, dedicated specially to the enjoyment of art. Human works in earlier times had a less specialised function in a wider social context – for example, as images of gods in temples, as adornment for the tombs of dead kings, as music for banquets and dancing. Art was 'utility art' before it became 'art'.

When, in conjunction with a push towards broader democratisation and the corresponding widening of the art market, the balance of power between art producers and art consumers gradually tilts in favour of the former, we finally reach a situation of the kind which can be observed in some branches of art in the twentieth century – especially in painting but also in elite music and even in popular music. In this case the dominant social canon of art is so constituted that the individual artist has far greater scope for self-regulated, individual experimentation and improvisation. In manipulating the symbolic forms of his art, he is far more free than the craft artist to follow his own personal understanding of their sequential patterns, their expressiveness and his own highly individualised feelings and taste. Here the work of art depends in large measure on individuals' self-questioning as to what pleases them personally in their materialised fantasies and experiments, and on their ability sooner or later to awaken a resonance in other people through these symbolic structures. The collective pressure of tradition and the tightly knit local society on the production of the art-work is reduced; the self-constraint by the individual art producer's conscience increases.

The same applies to the resonance produced by the work. The occasions on which works of art – such as organ music at a religious service or paintings as palace ornamentation – are addressed to groups of people assembled for other purposes grow less frequent in the fields of painting, music and literature.[2] At this stage the work of art is directed more than previously at a public of isolated individuals – such as the loosely integrated multiplicity of a metropolitan concert audience or the mass of visitors to a museum, each of whom goes alone, or at most in isolated couples, from picture to picture. Securely insulated from each other, each of them questions himself or herself as to the resonance of the work, asking if they personally like it and what they feel about it. In both the production and the reception of art an important part is played not only by highly individualised feelings but by a high degree of self-observation. Both bear witness to a high level of self-awareness. In some works, such as Picasso's variations on Velasquez's painting of the Spanish Infanta, the problem of artistic self-awarenss is clearly involved in the shaping of the work. In such cases the art recipient's awareness that his or her own individual response is a relevant aspect of every work is particularly pronounced.[3]

In this phase of the development of art, therefore, individual artists (Picasso, Schoenberg) or even small groups of artists (expressionists, atonalists) have greater importance as leaders of artistic taste. Again and again a few artists rush far ahead of the canon of art understanding in their field and

2 In architecture, and therefore sculpture, they are more prevalent, although examples like Le Corbusier or the Bauhaus show that in certain phases of the development of architecture innovative specialists can play a very important role as pace-setters for public taste.

3 The development indicated by the use of the terms 'objective' and 'subjective' to characterise different musical styles is of relevance here. It has two pre-conditions: first, a shift in the balance of power in favour of artists, allowing them to use their music to a higher degree as a means of expressing individual feelings; and second, a change in the structure of the music-loving public, involving an increase of individualisation. The recipients of 'subjective' music, too, were more concerned than at the time of 'objective' musical styles that music should arouse, give voice to their very personal feelings, and perhaps to suppressed feelings.

– whatever the difficulties of reception may be – they do not fail as a result. The word has got round that artists are prone to 'wild' or at least unusual behaviour, that they invent new forms that the public at first fails to perceive as such and therefore to understand; this is almost a part of the artist's job.

Of course, to begin with it is often very difficult to distinguish between successful and unsuccessful innovations in art. The enticingly wide scope for individual invention opens the door to failed experiments and unformed fantasies. In other words, the more differentiated, relatively developed societies have cultivated a comparatively high tolerance for highly individualised ways of further developing the existing art canon; this facilitates experimentation and the breaching of stale conventions and can thus help to enrich the artistic pleasures available through seeing and hearing. Admittedly, this is not without costs and risks. De-routinisation can itself congeal into convention. But in general the difficulties of communication that artistic innovations entail are more easily absorbed. They may give rise to conflicts; but there are social agencies (art historians, journalists, critics, essayists) who try to bridge the gaps, to soften the impact of artistic adventures and ease the transition to unfamiliar ways of hearing and seeing. If many artistic experiments turn out to be no more than stimulants or failures, experimentation has value in itself, although only a limited number of innovators pass the test of repeated acceptance by several generations.

Among the most interesting unanswered questions of our time is that of the structural characteristics on the basis of which the products of a particular person survive the selection process of a series of generations and are gradually absorbed into the canon of socially accepted works of art, while those of other people lapse into the shadowy world of forgotten works.

The Artist in the Human Being

Mozart is among the artists whose works have passed the ever-renewed test of generations especially convincingly. This is not true without reservations. Many of the compositions of his childhood and youth are now forgotten or arouse little response. The great curve of his social existence – the prodigy pampered by the high society of Europe, the more difficult fame of his industrious twenties and early thirties, the loss of popularity, especially in Vienna, the growing indigence and the isolation of his last years, then the very uneven rise of his fame after his death – all that is well enough known and does not need to be discussed in detail here. What is surprising, perhaps, is that Mozart survived his dangerous phase as a child prodigy without his talent being destroyed.

One not infrequently comes across the idea that the maturing of a talent of 'genius' is an autonomous, 'inner' process that takes place more or less in isolation from the human fate of the individual concerned. This idea is bound up with the other common notion that the creation of great works of art is independent of the social existence of their creator, of his or her development and experience as a human being among others. In keeping with this, biographers of Mozart often assume that the understanding of

Mozart the artist, and thus of his art, can be divorced from the understanding of Mozart the man. This separation is artificial, deceptive and unnecessary. Although the present state of knowledge does not allow us to lay bare the connections between the social existence and the works of an artist as if with a scalpel, it is possible to probe them in some depth.[1]

At the present stage of civilisation the transfiguration of the mysterious element in genius may satisfy a deeply-felt need. At the same time, it is one of many forms of the deification of 'great' people, the other side of which is contempt for ordinary people. By elevating the former above the human measure, one depresses the latter below it. Our understanding of an artist's achievement and the joy taken in his or her works is not diminished but is reinforced and deepened if we attempt to grasp the connection between the works and the artist's fate in the society of his or her fellows. The special gift or, as it was called in Mozart's day, the 'genius' a person has but is not, is itself one of the elements determining his or her social fate, and is to that extent a social fact, just like the simple gifts of people without genius.

In Mozart's case – unlike that of Beethoven, for example – the relation of the 'man' to the 'artist' has been

---

1 One of the peculiarities of the literature on Mozart is the fact that even a writer who sets out like St George to slay the dragon of the idealising cult of genius and to make the treasure available, pure and unfalsified, to mankind, turns out to be at bottom another worshipper of idols. Seldom has the idea of a man who develops into a great artist entirely from 'within', independently of his human fate, been elaborated on a higher level of reflection by a Mozart biographer than by Wolfgang Hildesheimer; and he does so, it seems to me, because of the same misunderstanding of 'human greatness' that he attacks in other biographies. The following quotation will serve as a brief example (*op. cit.*, p. 48): 'Surely, Mozart's development as a musician cannot be reduced to his increasing facility. Rather, like every great artist, he develops by gradually sounding the depths of his potential world, and conquering it, according to an inner law. This is especially true of Mozart, in that all his experience found its way exclusively into his work, not into the development of his personality, or into a maturation process, or verbally expressed wisdom, or a world view.' Poor Mozart! His music can mature without Mozart the man undergoing any process of maturation. A personality only reveals its development by uttering words of wisdom, by elaborating a comprehensive philosophical world view as well as operas and fantasies. One wonders if this is not a little narrow-minded. What harsh, intellectual inhumanity, what lack of empathy and compassion for a non-intellectual person speaks from these words!

---

especially confusing for many scholars, because the picture of him that emerges from letters, reports and other evidence assorts ill with the preconceived ideal of a genius. Mozart was a simple man, not particularly impressive if one met him in the street, sometimes childish and in private conversation far from sparing in the use of metaphors relating to excreta. From an early age he had a strong need of love, which manifested itself in the short years of his manhood both in the physical urge and in the constant desire for the affection of his wife and his public. The question is how someone equipped with all the animal needs of an ordinary human being could produce music which seemed to those who heard it devoid of all animality. Such music is characterised by terms such as 'deep', 'sensitive', 'sublime' or 'mysterious' – it seems to be part of a world different from that of ordinary experience, in which the mere recollection of less sublime aspects of human beings has a debasing effect.

The reason why this Romantic dichotomy has survived so tenaciously is clear. It is a reflection of the ever-renewed conflict between civilised people and their animality, which has never been properly resolved in all the stages of development up to now. The idealising image of the genius is enlisted as an ally of the forces that individuals marshal on behalf of their spirituality against their bodily self. The battlefield is displaced. The resulting division, whereby the mystery attributed to a genius on one hand and his or her ordinary humanity on the other are consigned to separate pigeon-holes, expresses an inhumanity deeply rooted in the European intellectual tradition. This is an unsolved problem of civilisation.

Every advance of civilisation, no matter where or on what level of human development it takes place, represents an attempt by human beings in their dealings with each other to pacify the untamed animal impulses which are a part of their natural endowment by means of countervailing socially generated impulses, or to sublimate and transform them culturally. This enables people to live with each other and with themselves without being constantly exposed to the uncontrollable pressure of their animal impulses – their own and those of others. If people remained, as they grew up, the same instinctive beings they were as children, their chances of survival would be extremely slight. They would be without learned means of orientation in their search for food, they would be helplessly susceptible to each momentary urge, and would thus be a permanent burden and a danger to themselves and others.

But the social canons and methods by which people build up instinct controls in their communal life are not brought into being deliberately; they evolve over long periods, blindly and without plan. Irregularities and contradictions in drive-controls, huge fluctuations in their severity or leniency, are therefore among the recurrent structural features of the civilising process. We encounter whole groups of people, or just individual people, who develop extreme forms of regulation of their animal impulses, who are inclined to wall up their impulses and to combat, with an immense expenditure of energy, people who do not do likewise. We also come across people who do the opposite, forming a very loose structure of instinct controls and impatiently trying to satisfy momentary impulses. Something of the former type's civilisatory over-reaction against instinct is still detectable in a canon of thought whose exponents are ready to divide humanity into two abstract categories, denoted by labels such as 'nature' and 'culture' or 'body' and 'mind', without the least attempt to investigate the connection between the phenomena to which these concepts refer. The same applies to the tendency to draw a sharp dividing line between artist and human being, genius and 'ordinary person'. It applies to the tendency to treat art as something floating in mid-air, outside and independently of the social lives of people.

Undoubtedly, there are characteristics of the human arts, particularly music, which encourage such an attitude. To begin with, there are processes of sublimation whereby human fantasies, converted into musical creations, can be divested of their animality without necessarily forfeiting their elementary dynamic, their impetus and strength, or the anticipated sweetness of fulfilment. Many of Mozart's works bear witness to an extraordinary transforming power of this kind.

A second feature of music, and of art in general – particularly in the complex, highly specialised form it takes in more developed societies – contributes to this tendency for it to be seen in isolation from its human context. Its resonance is clearly not confined to contemporary members of the society to which its creator belongs. It is one of the most significant characteristics of the human products we call 'works of art' that they are relatively autonomous in relation to their producer and their producer's society. Often enough, a work of art is only perceived as a masterpiece when it begins to strike a chord in people coming after the producer's generation. What qualities of a work, and what structural features of the social existence and the society of its creator, cause the creator to be regarded as 'great' by later generations – sometimes despite a lack of resonance among his or her contemporaries? This is an open question which is still often disguised as an eternal mystery today.

However, the relative autonomy of the work of art and the complex of problems associated with it do not relieve us of the obligation to investigate the connection between the experience and the fate of the creative artist in his or her society, that is, between this society itself and the works produced by the artist.

The relevance of this problem to our theme is greater than it might appear at first glance. The problem is not confined to music, or even to art. Clarification of the connections between an artist's experience and his or her work is also important for an understanding of ourselves as human beings. It makes the truism that people make music and enjoy listening to it, and do so at all stages of human development from the simplest to the most complex, seem somewhat less obvious and familiar. It replaces this idea by the larger question as to the special nature of those beings who have all the structural features of highly developed animals and are at the same time able to create, and respond to, magical forms, musical enchantments such as Mozart's *Don Giovanni* or his last three symphonies. Despite its sociological significance, the problem of the human capacity for sublimation has been somewhat neglected, as compared with the capacity for repression. In the present context, even if we cannot solve it, we are inevitably confronted by this question.

In talking about Mozart we find ourselves all too readily using terms like 'innate genius' or 'inborn ability to compose'; but these are thoughtless expressions. If we say that a feature of a person is inborn, we imply that it is genetically determined, biologically inherited in the same way as hair or eye colour. But it is simply impossible for a person to have a natural, genetically rooted propensity for anything as artificial as Mozart's music. Even before his twentieth birthday Mozart had written a large number of pieces in the special style that was fashionable at European courts at that time. With the facility that made him famous as a prodigy among his contemporaries, he composed exactly the kind of music that had emerged in his society, and only there, as a result of a peculiar development – that is to say, sonatas, serenades, symphonies, masses, etc. His ability to manipulate the complex musical instruments of his time – Mozart's father describes how effortlessly he learned to play the organ at the age of seven[2] – cannot have been genetically inherited any more than his mastery of these musical forms.

That Mozart's imagination expressed itself in sound patterns with a spontaneity and energy reminiscent of a natural force is beyond doubt. But if a force of nature was at work here, it was certainly a much less specific force than the one that manifested itself in the particular idiom of his prolific inventions. Mozart's extraordinary facility in composing and playing music conforming to the social music

2 Letter of 11 June 1763: I, p. 71.

canon of his time can be explained only as an expression of a sublimating transformation of natural energies, not as an expression of natural or inborn energies per se. If a biological predisposition played a part in his special talent, it can only have been a highly general, unspecific predisposition, for which we do not at present have even an adequate term.

It is conceivable, for example, that biological differences are involved in differing capacities for sublimation. In that sense one could imagine that Mozart possessed to an unusually high degree an innate, constitutional capacity to come to terms with the difficulties in early childhood that everyone has to contend with, through sublimation in the form of musical fantasies. But even that is a risky assumption. The reasons why particular mechanisms like projection, repression, identification or sublimation are preferred in the development of a particular personality are hardly known. No one will seriously doubt that even as a young child Mozart displayed a particularly strong ability to transform instinctual energies by sublimation. Nothing is taken away from Mozart's greatness or importance, or the joy communicated by his works, if that is said. On the contrary, here is a bridge over the fatal abyss that opens if one tries to separate Mozart the artist from the man.

However, to understand this unity, we need to go a few steps further. There cannot be many steps, as the question of sublimation is relatively unexplored.

Among the factors which clearly influence the process of sublimation are the extent and direction of sublimation in the parents of a child, or in other adults with whom the child has close contact in early life. Later, too, models of sublimation, such as suitable teachers, can exert a decisive influence through their personalities. Furthermore, one often has the impression that a person's position in the chain of generations has a special influence on the likelihood of sublimation; in other words, sublimation is easier for people in the second or third generation.

Mozart's father was a man with a pronounced pedagogic tendency. He was a gifted musician of the middle rank, and not unknown among his contemporaries as the author of a violin tutor. An ambitious, intelligent craftsman's son with a broad education, he had achieved a certain success as deputy conductor at the Salzburg court, but not enough to satisfy his aspirations. His whole desire for fulfilment in his social existence was thus focused on his children, above all his son. For him his son's musical education eclipsed all other tasks, including his own profession. Not enough is known about Mozart's relationship to his mother; but this situation with a musician father seeking fulfilment for an urgent, unsatisfied yearning through his son, is a not unfavourable constellation for a resolution of early childhood conflicts through sublimation. Thus Leopold Mozart greeted his son's first attempts at composition with tears in his eyes. A strong bond of love formed between him and his son, who was rewarded for each musical achievement with a big prize in terms of affection. This undoubtedly favoured the child's development in the direction desired by his father. More will be said later about these connections.

It may be useful to explore in somewhat more detail the peculiar ability of Mozart's that we have in mind when we call him a 'genius'. To be sure, it would be better to avoid this Romantic concept. What it means is not difficult to define. It means that Mozart could do something that the great majority of people are unable to do, which is beyond their powers of imagination: Mozart could give free rein to his fantasies. They poured out in a flood of sound-patterns which, when heard by other people, stimulated their feelings in the most diverse ways. The decisive factor in this was that while his imagination expressed itself in combinations of forms that stayed within the framework of the social canon of music which he had assimilated, these forms went far beyond the combinations previously known and the feelings they conveyed. It is this ability to produce innovations in the field of sound which convey a potential or actual message to others, produce a resonance in them, that we attempt to pin down with concepts such as 'creativity' as applied to music and, *mutatis mutandis*, to art in general.

In using such terms one is frequently unaware that most people are capable of producing innovative fantasies. Many dreams are of this kind. 'I've just dreamed something extraordinary', people sometimes say. 'It's as if someone quite different from me was dreaming,' so a young girl expressed it, 'I have no idea how I get such ideas.' The point at issue here has nothing to do with dream contents. The pioneering work done by Freud and some of his pupils in this area is untouched by it. Here we are concerned with the creative side of dream-work. New and often quite incomprehensible connections are revealed in dreams.[3]

But the innovative fantasies of dreaming people, and even daydreams, differ in a specific way from the fantasies that become a work of art. They are usually chaotic, or at least disordered and confused and, although often of burning interest to the dreamer, of little or no interest to other people. The peculiarity of innovatory fantasies in the form of works of art is that they are fantasies kindled by material which is accessible to many people. In a word, they are de-privatised fantasies. That sounds simple, but the whole difficulty of artistic creation shows itself when someone tries to cross this bridge – the bridge of de-privatisation. It could also be called the bridge of sublimation. To take such a step people must be able to subordinate the power of fantasy expressed in their personal night-dreams or daydreams to the intrinsic regularities of the material, so that their products are cleansed of all purely I-related residues. In other words, in addition to their I-relevance, they must give their fantasies you-, he-, she-, we- and they-relevance. It is to meet this requirement that the fantasies are subordinated

---

3   The libido stream flows through the cells of our memories and manipulates the stored forms and events like a practised theatre director, driving them forth in new scenes. Who writes the scenarios of our dreams? A half-automatic part of ourselves, director and actor at once, it transforms the material of our memories, makes something new from it, links it up in scenes we have never experienced.

to a material, whether of words, colours, stone, sounds or whatever else.

In addition, the influx of fantasies into a material without loss of spontaneity, dynamism or innovatory force, requires capabilities that go beyond mere fantasising in a given material. It needs a thorough familiarity with the intrinsic regularities of the material, a comprehensive training in handling them and an extensive knowledge of their properties. This training, the acquisition of this knowledge, brings certain dangers with it. It can impair the strength and spontaneity of the fantasies; in other words, it can infringe *their* intrinsic dynamics. Instead of developing them further by applying them to the material, one can completely paralyse them. For the transforming, de-animalising, civilising of the elemental fantasy-stream by the knowledge-stream and, if all goes well, the final merging of the two as the material is manipulated is, in part, the resolution of a conflict. The acquired knowledge, which includes acquired thinking or, in the reified language of tradition, 'reason', or, in Freudian terms, the 'ego', opposes the more animal energy-impulses when they try to take control of the skeletal muscles and thus of action. That these libidinal impulses also flow through the chambers of memory in their effort to control human action, kindling the fire of dream fantasies in them – that in the work of the artist they are purified by a stream of knowledge until they finally merge with it – therefore represents a reconciliation between originally antagonistic tendencies of the personality.

And there is something else. The creation of a work of art, the manipulation of the material concerned, is an open-ended process; the artist is advancing along a path that he or she has never trodden before and, in the case of the great master, that no one has trodden before. Art creators experiment. They test their fantasies on the material, on the material of their fantasy which is constantly taking new shape. At every moment they have the possibility of going either here or there. They can go off the rails, and say to themselves as they step back: 'That doesn't work, doesn't sound right, doesn't look right. That's facile, trivial, falls apart, doesn't link up into a taut, integrated structure.' It is therefore not only the internal dynamics of the fantasy-stream, nor only the knowledge stream that are involved in the production of an art-work, but also a controlling element of the personality, the producer's artistic conscience, a voice that says: 'This is how it should be; like this it looks right, sounds right, feels right, and not like that.' If production moves along known paths, this individual conscience speaks with the voice of the social canon of art. But if artists develop the familiar canon further, as Mozart did in his later years, they must rely on their own artistic conscience. As they immerse themselves in their material they must take quick decisions as to whether the direction their spontaneous fantasy is taking them as they work on the material matches its immanent dynamics or not.

On this level, too, therefore, there is a reconciliation and fusion of two originally conflicting currents or tendencies within the artist – at least in societies where the production of art-works is a highly specialised and complex activity. These societies demand of their adult members a very extensive differentiation of their id, ego and super-ego functions. If the libidinal fantasy-stream flows relatively unchecked by knowledge and conscience into a material, artistic forms can appear dislocated and disconnected, as is seen, for example, in drawings by schizophrenics. Unsuitable elements, which only mean something to the creator, may be juxtaposed. The intrinsic regularities of the material, by means of which the artist's feelings and vision can be communicated to others, are clumsily used or violated, so that they are unable to perform their socialising function.

The pinnacle of artistic creation is achieved when the spontaneity and inventiveness of the fantasy-stream are so fused with knowledge of the regularities of the material and the judgement of the artist's conscience that the innovative fantasies emerge as if by themselves in a way that matches the demands of both material and conscience. This is one of the most socially fruitful types of sublimation process.[4]

Mozart is a representative of this type in its most clear-cut form. In his case the spontaneity of the fantasy-stream was largely unbroken by being converted into music. Often enough musical inventions flowed from him as dreams emanate from a sleeping person. Some reports suggest that while he was in the company of other people he would sometimes be secretly listening to a piece of music that was taking shape within him. He would then hastily excuse himself, the reports say; after a while he would come back in good spirits. He had just, as we say, 'composed' one of his works.

The fact that at such times a work composed itself, so to speak, by itself was the result not only of the intimate fusion of his fantasy-stream with his craftsman's knowledge of the timbre and range of the instruments of his time or the traditional forms of music. It also sprang from the union of both, knowledge and fantasy, with his highly developed and extremely sensitive artistic conscience. What we feel to be the perfection of many of his works is due equally to his rich imagination, his comprehensive knowledge of the musical material and the spontaneity of his musical conscience. However great the innovations of his musical fantasy, he never struck a wrong note. He knew with somnambulistic certainty which sound-figures – within the framework of the social canon in which he worked – conformed to the immanent dynamics of the music he wrote, and which he had to reject.

The inspiration comes. Sometimes it unrolls by itself like the dreams of a sleeper, leaving its trace more or less completely on the recorder we call 'memory', so that the artist can inspect his own ideas like a spectator viewing the

4 To refer to this transformation of libidinal forces as a 'defence mechanism' is to indicate only one of its functions. In psychoanalytical terminology one might say that through sublimation the three agencies that Freud describes as separate – ego, id and super-ego – are reconciled.

work of another. He can check them as if from a distance, elaborate and correct them or, if his artistic conscience falters, make them worse. Unlike dream ideas, those of the artist are attuned both to the material and to society. They are a specific form of communication, intended to elicit applause, resonance of a positive or negative kind, to arouse joy or anger, clapping or booing, love or hate.

This simultaneous attunement both to the material and to society, the connection between which may not be apparent at first sight, is far from accidental. Each of the materials characteristic of a particular artistic field has its own inexhaustible regularities and a corresponding resistance to the will of the creator. If an art-work is to come into being the personal fantasy-stream must be so transformed that it can be represented in one of these materials. The art producer – no matter how spontaneous the fusion of fantasy and material may be – has constantly to resolve the tensions that arise between them. Only then can fantasy take on form, become an integral part of a work and thereby become communicable, able to produce a response in others, if not necessarily in the contemporaries of the artist.

This also means, however, that no artist is ever a wholly effortless creator of works of art, not even Mozart. The extremely high degree of fusion between his fantasy-stream and the immanent dynamics of his material, the astonishing ease with which long sequences of sound-figures came into his consciousness, their inventiveness blending as if of its own accord with the immanent ordering of their sequential structure, by no means always dispensed Mozart from the task of working the material over under the eye of his conscience. All the same, he is said to have remarked once, late in his life, that it was easier for him to compose than not to do so.[5]

This is a revealing statement, and there is good reason to believe it authentic. At first sight it may sound like the

5 Letter of September 1791 to da Ponte (its authenticity has been questioned): Hildesheimer, *op. cit.*, p. 193.

utterance of a favourite of the gods. Only on looking more closely do we find that we have before us a very painful admission by a tormented man.[6]

Perhaps this brief discussion of the personality structures that were at work in a person as astonishing as Mozart, and not only in him, may do something to make the familiar way of talking about Mozart the man and Mozart the artist as if they were two different people seem less plausible. Once, Mozart the man was idealised to make him fit in with the preconceived idea of a genius. Now there is sometimes a tendency to treat Mozart the artist as a kind of superman and Mozart the man with slight contempt. That is not a judgement that he deserves. It rests not least on the idea mentioned earlier that his musical ability was an inherited gift of nature, with no connection to the rest of his personality. It may help to correct such ideas by recalling the extensive musical knowledge and highly developed conscience that were bound up inseparably with his musical creation. Many standard comments on Mozart that we meet in this context, assertions such as 'Mozart simply did not understand himself', reinforce the idea that artistic conscience is one of the inborn functions of a person, and therefore of Mozart. But conscience, whatever its specific form, is innate to no one. At most the potential for forming a conscience is a natural human endowment. This potential is activated and shaped into a specific structure through a person's life with others. The individual conscience is society-specific. This is seen in Mozart's artistic conscience, its attunement to a music as peculiar as that of court society.

---

6 Mozart, in his unsatisfied desire for love, suffered much and dealt with his suffering by creating works which were sometimes graceful and playful, and sometimes deeply moving. That he failed to achieve the desired success with them was due not least to his extremely strict conscience. Mozart felt his gift, of which he was very conscious, as an obligation, and he refused to betray it even when this would have made his life easier. Of course, that was not entirely his decision. It was partly an unconscious compulsion, but it was *also* a decision. And because he unhesitatingly followed his conscience beyond the point where he jeopardised the response and thus forfeited the love and applause of the public that he also needed, because of this he deserves – as a man who was an artist – the admiration and gratitude of posterity.

The Formative Years of a Genius

No one can presume today to answer the question how a talent as extraordinary as Mozart's came into being. But one can define the question somewhat more sharply, and indicate directions in which answers may be found. In this respect, too, the individual case has paradigmatic significance. The question how a singular creative talent comes about concerns everyone to some degree.

Mozart had a very unusual childhood. He is still seen today as the prodigy *par excellence*. In his fourth year he was able to learn and play fairly complex pieces of music in a very short time under his father's direction. At five he began to compose. Before his sixth birthday his father took him and his sister on their first concert tour to Munich, where both children performed before the Bavarian Elector Maximilian III. Later, in autumn 1762, the three Mozarts went to Vienna, where they played at the imperial court and elsewhere. Wolfgang Mozart was delicate and sickly, but he was praised and admired everywhere for his extraordinary musical skill. The enormous success Leopold Mozart had in showing his children, especially his son, performing in Vienna, induced him to organise a 'world tour' around the courts and palaces of Europe.

From a sociological point of view, the Mozart family's concert tours show their peculiar and in some respects unique situation as outsiders. From their Salzburg backwater where the court trumpeter and the pastry cook were among their closer acquaintances, they were suddenly projected, first on the trip to Vienna, into the highest reaches of society. On 16 October 1762 Mozart's father wrote home that the young Count Palfi had attended the six-year-old's concert at Linz. Through him news of the child's stay reached the empress; hence the invitation to give a concert at court. Leopold Mozart describes the event as follows:

> Now all that I have time for is to say in great haste that Their Majesties received us with such extraordinary graciousness that, when I shall tell of it, people will declare that I have made it up. Suffice it to say that Wolferl jumped upon the Empress's lap, put his arms round her neck and kissed her heartily. In short, we were there from three to six o'clock and the Emperor himself came out of the next room and made me go in there to hear the Infanta play the violin. On the 15th the Empress sent us by the Privy Paymaster, who drove up to our house in state, two dresses, one for the boy and one for the girl. As soon as the command arrives, they are to appear at court and the Privy Paymaster will fetch them. Today at half past two in the afternoon they are to go to the two yongest Archdukes and at four o'clock to the Hungarian Chancellor, Count Palffy. Yesterday we were with Count Kaunitz, and the day before with Countess Kinsky and later with the Court von Ulefeld. And we already have more engagements for the next two days.[1]

So it goes on, day after day. The Empress has 100 ducats paid to Mozart's father through her paymaster; a single academy brings in 6 ducats, some high lords and ladies for whom the children perform finally only part with 2. On 19 October Leopold Mozart sends a merchant friend 120 ducats to be invested safely, but part of the money is to be

1 *LMF*, p. 6.

used to buy a carriage 'to give the children greater comfort'.[2] For the six-year-old boy this tour, like all the later ones, is exhausting work. He goes down with scarlet fever, the concerts have to be interrupted for a time. He can stay in bed and rest.

This is a small sample of the life the Mozart family, specially the father and son, are to lead – with interruptions – up to the latter's twenty-first year.

When his son was seven, therefore, Leopold Mozart took him, with his wife and daughter, on a grand tour of Europe. They were away for more than three years. Wherever they appeared the two children, especially the boy, caused a sensation. He played the piano like a grown-up, performed all the tricks that were asked of him, playing with the keyboard covered or with one finger. He was constantly in close contact with the 'great ones' of the earth. In Paris and London the whole family was invited to court. All this was stimulating and astonishing for the child, but it was also hard work. At each place their father arranged as many performances as could be crammed in. And they brought in money. For how could he have paid for the tour except with the income from the concerts? Just like the concert tours of contemporary virtuosi, the trip was a commercial undertaking. At the same time, for himself and his son, it was a source of complete fulfilment.

All the same, what he or the children received was usually at the discretion of the noble assemblies before whom they appeared. In those days the payment of an artist, a virtuoso, was still treated as an *ex gratia* gift, in the absolutist court tradition. The amount could never be predicted; it depended on the generosity of the prince or nobles before whom one had played. Some were munificent, others – the majority – fell short of Leopold Mozart's expectations. To begin with, his letters give the impression that profits from the life of travelling musicians at the courts and palaces of Europe were very satisfactory. For a time the family prospered. But

2 *LMF*, p. 7.

as the prodigies grew older their fame soon wore off. On their second visit to Paris and Vienna their reception was noticeably cooler than on the first, the takings correspondingly lower. Even so, the trip, which ended with their return to Salzburg on 29 November 1766, seems to have brought the family a bigger income than they earned in Salzburg.

In 1767 the Mozarts again travelled to Vienna, where they were caught up in a smallpox epidemic. They had an audience with Empress Maria Theresa and her son, Joseph II. Father Mozart seized on the emperor's suggestion that his son should compose an opera – largely because he hoped this would finally silence envious voices. The twelve-year-old Mozart wrote his first opera buffa in the spring and summer of 1768 (*La finta semplice*); however, its performance was blocked by the theatre management. In the late summer of the same year he wrote the Singspiel *Bastien and Bastienne*, which was given its first performance soon after in the garden theatre of the famous Dr Mesmer. This time the family was away from Salzburg for barely a year and a half, until January 1769.

In 1770 father and son set off for Italy, where the young Mozart enjoyed new triumphs. He passed an exam at the Accademia filarmonica di Bologna that would have been difficult enough for most adult musicians, and began writing an opera seria for the theatre at Bologna, which had its first performance in Milan in December (*Mitridate, Re di Ponto*). In March 1771 father and son returned to Salzburg, but in August they set off – Mozart was now fifteen – on a second trip to Italy, and were back in Salzburg by the end of the year. Although Leopold Mozart had a post as deputy conductor at the Salzburg court, the old prince-bishop was indulgent as long as he did not have to pay him his salary while he was away. After his death in 1772 a new lord came to Salzburg as prince-bishop, Count Jerome Colloredo, who imposed a stricter regime.

The period from 1756 to 1777 could perhaps be called Mozart's years of apprenticeship. If we look more closely at this time, we find evaporating before our eyes the idea that 'genius' was present from the first, independently of the experiences of Mozart's youth, following only its inner regularities and coming to maturity in works such as *Don Giovanni* or the Jupiter Symphony. It becomes clear that the peculiarity of his childhood and his years of apprenticeship are indissolubly bound up with the peculiarities of Mozart's person that are referred to by the concept of genius.

What sort of picture do we get of the young Mozart? Among the earliest evidence we have is an account of the child's unusual aural sensibility and his intense, hyper-sensitive need for love. A friend of the family, the Salzburg court trumpeter Schachtner, tells us: 'Even childish games had to be accompanied by music if they were to interest him. When we carried toys from one room to another, the one of us who carried nothing had to sing a march or play the fiddle.' And: 'Almost until his tenth year he had an unconquerable fear of the trumpet, if it was played on its own without other instruments. If you just held a trumpet in front of him it was as if you held a loaded pistol to his heart.' [3] His oversensitive need for love is also described by this witness: 'Because I paid attention to him ... he was so fond of me that he would often ask me ten times in a day whether I liked him. And if I occasionally said no, just as a joke, there would be tears shining in his eyes.'[4]

It seems that Mozart's need for love had grown uncertain of itself in early childhood. His feeling of being unloved found constant confirmation in his changing experiences over the years, and the intensity of his unsatisfied desire to be loved, detectable as a dominant wish throughout his life, very largely determined what had meaning for him and what did not. As a child he needed constant reassurance that he

---

3 *Mozart. Die Dokumente seines Lebens*, collected and annotated by Otto Erich Deutsch. Basle/London/New York 1961, p. 395. Cf. Erich Schenk: *Mozart, sein Leben – seine Welt*, 2nd ed., Vienna/Munich 1975, pp. 48–51.
4 *Ibid.*, pp. 395f.

was loved, and if this need went unsatisfied he openly showed his sadness and despair. His special sensitivity, his vulnerability to rejection, is very clear in Schachtner's recollections. He seems to have been quite defenceless against it.

As a grown man he was hardly less sensitive and vulnerable. The search for proofs of love, for friendship and affection, behind which one senses a measure of self-hate, a feeling of not being lovable, remained one of his dominant traits. In a letter telling his father of his forthcoming marriage to Constanze Weber, he finishes the sentence ending 'and she loves me with all her heart' with a question mark, no doubt added inadvertently.[5] In another letter, to his wife, he quotes a line from his *Magic Flute*: 'Death and despair were his reward' – the reward, that is, of the man who placed his trust in women.[6]

In these later years Mozart strove to conceal his vulnerability. He protected himself from it with often coarse and sombre humour, but above all by forgetting, by not perceiving, by a manifest indifference to slights and defeats. And then, of course, there was his music, especially composing. It may be that his music already helped him over his difficulties at an early age. For long periods it undoubtedly earned him love and admiration. When the feeling of being unloved and lonely got too strong, it must have been a comfort and a refuge. By the end, however, he could no longer shut his eyes; his failure, the unfulfilment of his need for love, the meaninglessness of his life were inescapable. So he gave up and died – apparently without success, while success and fame awaited him around the next corner.

Mozart's father, himself a musician, taught the child to play the piano probably in his third year. A faint hope of achieving the desired social advancement that he had only partly fulfilled by his own efforts may have awakened in him

5   15 December 1781: *LMF*, p. 784. Cf. Hildesheimer: *op. cit.*, p. 253.
6   11 June 1791: *LMF*, p. 954. Cf. Hildesheimer, *op. cit.*, p, 321.

very early on. He undoubtedly devoted far more time to the little boy than was usual. Leopold Mozart took possession of his son and, as the prodigy's father, led the life that had been denied to him up to then. For twenty years, up to the start of his journey to Paris with his mother, Mozart lived – and travelled – almost constantly with his father. He was always with him, always under his eyes and his protection. He clearly never went to school. His whole education, his early musical training, his knowledge of languages and culture – all were acquired with his father's help and according to his precepts.

There is therefore good reason to say that Leopold Mozart tried to achieve the previously absent fulfilment of his life through his son. There is no point in asking whether he was right to do so. When their life's fulfilment is at stake, people are often ruthless. For twenty years the father worked on his son, almost like a sculptor on his sculpture – on the 'prodigy' whom, as he was wont to declare, God had sent him in his mercy, and who might not have become what he was without his father's untiring work. In September 1777 he had to watch his son set off for distant parts for the first time without accompanying him, as he would otherwise have lost his position under the next prince-bishop. On the other hand, this journey to Paris, which he was financing, was absolutely necessary to his own hopes for the future. So, caught between conflicting compulsions, he sent at least Wolfgang's mother with him, while he stayed behind utterly dejected, as he writes, with symptoms of illness and serious depression. Among the familiar figures in the psychotherapeutic scenario of our day is the 'possessive mother'. Less common, at least from our present viewpoint, is the possessive father. Leopold Mozart might serve as an example.

Again it must be added that this conclusion is merely a diagnostic hypothesis. Who could presume to judge in such matters? The aim is to gain a somewhat better understanding of a great man, Wolfgang Amadeus Mozart, to whom mankind owes much pleasure. This cannot be done entirely without considering the parents, and in this case especially the father.

Let us briefly recapitulate: Leopold Mozart came from a family of craftsmen. His father and brother were Augsburg bookbinders. It may give an idea of the status of the family to learn that when the young Mozart stopped in Augsburg on his journey to Paris and was received by a prominent patrician, Leopold's brother had to wait outside the house until his nephew re-appeared.[7]

How Leopold Mozart made his way from the status of a craftsman to that of a Salzburg court musician and deputy conductor need not be related here. It was a step forward – probably in his own eyes, too – but not a very big one, considerably less than he had hoped. He had written a violin tutor that was well received and made his name known, as well as a number of compositions which, by all accounts, were no better or worse than countless others. Under the lax regime of the old prince-bishop he had been reasonably satisfied with his work at Salzburg, although even before his son's birth he seems to have looked out – perhaps with the aid of the violin tutor – for a more elevated position at a larger and richer court. He found the stricter regime of Count Colloredo oppressive, in fact unbearable. But what was he to do? At bottom he was a proud man. He was well aware of his intellectual superiority to most of the court lackeys; he took a keen interest in the wider political events of his time and, as his letters show, he had an astonishing power to observe and understand what was going on in the courts of the world.

His son Wolfgang wrote to him on the way to Paris that he hated toadying.[8] And indeed, that is one of Mozart's most striking features: however much he frequented aristocratic and court circles he did not dance attendance, did not flatter or crawl. Leopold Mozart was probably no less proud. But,

7   Mozart's letter of 14 October 1777: II, p. 54.
8   Letter of 10 December 1777: II, p. 179; his father's reply: II, p. 191. Cf. the letters from Wolfgang's weeks of emancipation from father and prince-bishop (May/June 1781): III, p. 115, 127.

if the father was not to revert to artisan status or find himself on the streets, he had hardly any other choice than playing the courtier – and *how* he did it is best seen in his portrait of 1765, with the somewhat grim mouth and the mistrustful eyes.[9] He had to bow and scrape, flatter and grovel, although he rejected this charge when it came from his son. He sometimes flattered in such an exaggerated way that one senses the constraint behind it. Father Mozart was better than his son at affecting a courtier's manner, but it had not become second nature to him.

The person we meet in his letters is a man with a specifically bourgeois outlook, whose wisdom and insight are often in contradiction to his bitterness, his black depressions, his panic fear and his bad conscience. Not a simple man. He espoused the doctrines of the Enlightenment and, after the unhoped-for recovery of his daughter from a grave illness, immediately had masses said in a number of churches in Salzburg, as he had no doubt promised the saints in his fear during the illness. He was a rationalist in the mould of his time, and at the same time drawn to the miraculous beliefs of the church, to which he remained devoted. He justified his plan of going on a concert tour with his two children by the anti-Enlightenment argument that he was obliged to 'announce to the world a miracle, which God has allowed to see the light in Salzburg. I owe this act to Almighty God, otherwise I should be the most thankless creature. *And if it is ever to be my duty to convince the world of this miracle, it is so now, when people are ridiculing whatever is called a miracle and denying all miracles.*'[10]

With regard to his son, too, it seems that he was at war with himself. Tormented by guilt, he often wavered between the self-appointed duty, which gave his life meaning, of making something 'great' of his son by unremitting work

9 Reproduced in Hildesheimer, *op. cit.*, after p. 152.
10 Letter of 30 July 1768: LMF, p. 89. Cf. Schenk, *op. cit.*, p. 54.

and discipline, and sympathy for the child, in which he was not lacking. An extract from another letter may make this clear:

> God, who has been far too good to me, a miserable sinner, has bestowed such talents on my children that, apart from my duty as a father, they alone would spur me on to sacrifice everything to their successful development. Every moment I lose is lost for ever. And if I ever guessed how precious for youth is time, I realise it now. You know that my children are accustomed to work. But if with the excuse that one thing prevents another they were to accustom themselves to hours of idleness, my whole plan would crumble to pieces. Habit is an iron shirt. And you yourself know how much my children and especially Wolfgang have to learn.[11]

He remarked once that he wanted to be not only his son's father but his best friend.[12] But at the same time he always managed to persuade him, by the superior power of argument, to do what he thought right. Leopold Mozart himself had been to a Jesuit school. In his treatment of his children, he was guided to some extent by models that were imprinted on his mind at school. As a man of the Enlightenment he did not beat his children. He replaced the stick by a means of chastisement no less effective – and no less painful: the intellect. In short, like many rationalists with a pedagogic gift he was in the habit of subjugating the taught to the personal will of the teacher by the cold logic of impersonal argument and his own more comprehensive knowledge.

In this school, therefore, Mozart grew up, tied to a father for whom the social and financial success of his son during his childhood and early youth represented his last and only chance of escaping an uncongenial situation and attaining meaning and fulfilment in his life.

11 10 November 1766: LMF, pp. 68–9. Cf. Wilhelm Zentner, *Der junge Mozart*, Altötting 1946, p. 67.
12 Letter of 20 July 1778: II, p. 413.

To an extent, the father's need for meaning matched the needs of his son, while he was small. His hope of achieving through his offspring what he had failed to achieve himself found a response in the strong need for love of the child, to whom the musical stimulus from his father clearly gave pleasure.

That the aural sensitivity of different people differs according to their natural constitution, that Mozart was gifted from birth with an unusual sensitivity to sounds, is quite possible, though incapable of proof in this case. What can be proved, and thus made more easy to understand, is the connection between the peculiar human constellation surrounding Mozart's childhood and youth, and the development of his special gift, and everything else that he found important for his fulfilment. The intense desire of a father prone to frequent feelings of guilt and depression for meaning and fulfilment through his young son, and the intense desire of an emotionally insecure child for love and affection, reinforced each other.

We do not know exactly what part the mother played in this constellation; there is not enough evidence. She was apparently a warm-hearted, vivacious and patient woman with some musical interests, the daughter of a family which had also risen from the artisan class. As far as we can see, she submitted unquestioningly and without great difficulty to her husband's authority, as was usual for women of her class. Wolfgang Mozart came from what might today be called a happy marriage of the old type: the husband took all the decisions, the wife followed him with absolute trust in his decency, his affection for her and the superiority of his intellect. The mother clearly identified herself entirely with her family; in her letters she sometimes says 'we' where one might expect 'I'.

A child who develops very pronounced faculties which meet his father's need for meaning, and a father whose affection and attention meet the child's need for meaning – this kind of double bind is certainly not uncommon. It appears especially clearly here because the needs of father and son fitted together so well at this early stage of their relationship. Each sign of musical talent in his son delighted the father. His delight was expressed in the intensity of his efforts to develop the child's talent further, in his constant concern with the child, the love and affection he lavished on him. And all this delighted the child, spurring him to new achievements that promised further love.

There can be little doubt that this double bind also involved negative feelings – particularly as quite openly ambivalent feelings are almost always found in young children. But the few sources we have from that time show above all the positive aspects. A biographer sums up the evidence as follows: 'He was touchingly attached to his "Papa". Each evening before bed he would climb on to his armchair, sing a melody from an Italian text with his father, and as a finale press a kiss on the tip of his progenitor's nose.'[13]

Many years later, when the son, in the infatuation of a great love, wants to break free of the double bind, his father reminds him of these childhood scenes in a desperate letter of warning. It is the year 1778 and Mozart is twenty-two. He has fallen head over heels in love with a seventeen-year-old girl, the elder sister of his future wife, and wants to abandon his father's planned trip to Paris to devote himself to training his beloved and taking her on a tour of Italy, where she will make a sensational impression as a singer. It is a harebrained plan; it threatens all the hopes the father has placed in his son's success in the French capital. Leopold Mozart tries as best he can to restrain his anger and despair at the younger man's senseless project and his disobedience. But he is himself tied to Salzburg, and his son is far off with his mother, in Mannheim. Only in letters can he keep some hold on the son who is slowly slipping out of his control. So he reminds him of those childhood scenes, in the many pages of his letter of 12 February 1778:

13 Zentner, *op. cit.*, p. 32.

My dear son, I implore you to read this letter carefully – and take time to reflect upon it. Merciful God! those happy moments are gone when, as child and boy, you never went to bed without standing on a chair and singing to me *Oragna fiagata fa*, and ending by kissing me again and again on the tip of my nose and telling me that when I grew old you would put me in a glass case and protect me from every breath of air, so that you might always have me with you and honour me. Listen to me, therefore, in patience! You are fully acquainted with our difficulties in Salzburg – you know my wretched income, why I kept my promise to let you go away, and all my various troubles. The purpose of your journey was twofold – either to get a good permanent appointment, or, if this should fail, to go off to some big city where large sums of money can be earned. Both plans were designed to assist your parents and to help on your dear sister, but above all to build up your own name and reputation in the world. The latter was partly accomplished in your childhood and boyhood; and it now depends on you alone to raise yourself gradually to a position of eminence, such as no musician has ever obtained. You owe that to the extraordinary talents which you have received from a beneficent God; and now it depends solely on your good sense and your way of life whether you die as an ordinary musician, utterly forgotten by the world, or as a famous Kapellmeister, of whom posterity will read, – whether, captured by some woman, you die bedded on straw in an attic full of starving children, or whether, after a Christian life spent in contentment, honour and renown, you leave this world with your family well provided for and your name respected by all.[14]

In his reply of 19 February Mozart says he never expected anything but his father's disapproval for the journey with the girl (and her family), and: 'Those days when, standing on a chair, I used to sing to you *Oragna fiagata fa* and finish by kissing you on the tip of your nose, are gone indeed; but do I honour, love and obey you any the less on that account? I

14 *LMF*, p, 475.

will say no more. As for your reproach about the little singer in Munich, I must confess that I was an ass. . .'[15] Soon after this he slips in the double-edged comment that he had come to Munich 'straight from Salzburg, where one loses the habit of contradicting'. It may have been said of the prince, but was doubtless meant for the father as well.

This letter clearly reflects the pressures Mozart felt weighing on him. The dominant desire to escape his feeling of confinement, in which financial hardship mingled with the need for respect and dignity, oppressed him no less than his unsatisfactory position at court. We can now more easily understand how it could come about that a few years after Mozart's birth his father could make his education the overriding purpose of his life. It is not surprising that the force driving the father, and the material pressure reinforcing it, should have been transmitted in a somewhat different form to the son.

The importance of being of the second generation, of growing up in a family which provides intense stimulus to the areas in which a person is gifted, has already been discussed. We do not know whether Mozart heard his father playing the violin in the first year of his life, but it is not unlikely. What is known is that from an early age he attended the daily piano lessons his father gave his elder sister Nannerl.

Soon the little brother tried his own hand at the piano. Sibling rivalry is one of the strongest impulses in early childhood. Like so many children in the same situation, the young Mozart may have fought for his share of his father's love and attention by imitating his rival, hitting the keys as she did. Noticing with pleasure his son's unusual early interest in the sound of the spinet, then in playing the violin, the father extended to him the loving interest that had seemed to the child previously reserved to his sister. That the son reacted to these pedagogical efforts by

15 *LMF*, p. 485.

absorbing the material with a speed and avidity far exceeding all his father's expectations, must have heightened the father's affection for his son. And this heightened affection spurred the son to still greater achievements.

What first amazed Leopold Mozart was his son's unusual speed of comprehension, to the development of which he must have unwittingly contributed much. The young Wolfgang's extraordinary aural acuity and memory, and the sureness of his musical understanding, seemed to Leopold quite genuinely a kind of miracle. The systematic tuition he gave his son from his third year reinforced this impression. It was a strict programme, with regular practice exercises according to a manual the father had compiled himself. The manuscript has survived. It contains 135 pieces, usually in minuet form, methodically arranged in terms of difficulty. Some of the child's earliest attempts at composition have also been preserved; they drew from his father 'tears of admiration and joy'.[16]

Astute and prudent as he was, Leopold Mozart recognised the opportunities that were opening up for him and his family. From now on he devoted his life to his son as father, friend, teacher and impresario. One expression of these activities was the long series of concert tours that has been described.

Mozart's was a hard schooling. What did it give him?

On the plus side of the account was the unique wealth of musical stimuli he received at home and on his tours. His father first sought to train his musical understanding in keeping with the traditions of his time. He started from the stock of musical knowledge that had become canonical. This suited his own taste and that of the public, on whose favour the success of the concert tours in particular depended. They did not want to be served anything exotic, combinations of notes the ear had to get used to. They wanted to hear pieces in the familiar style, perhaps in its

16 *Mozart. Die Dokumente seines Lebens*, p. 396.

latest form, but nothing difficult, over-individualised, taxing. In short, what was expected of young artists was pleasing, complaisant music. It could be difficult only as regards technique, not in its actual structure. Virtuosi were admired.

Mozart thus received from his father a very thorough traditional training. From the age of three to six he was introduced to works by most of the known composers in Austria and south Germany, and probably some north German ones as well. But on his tours he gained a much wider knowledge of the musical life of his time. In Paris he got to know works by Lully, Philidor, Johann Schobert and other well-known representatives of the French School. In London he encountered works by Handel, Johann Christian Bach and Karl Friedrich Abel, another pupil of Bach's. In Vienna he heard compositions by Georg Christoph Wagenseil and Georg Reutter, one of Haydn's teachers. In Italy he encountered Padre Martini, the leading master of counterpoint at the time. He heard the latest Italian operas and met many of their composers in person. He also got to know exponents of the Mannheim School. Joseph Haydn impressed him deeply; he learned much from Haydn, who for his part had the greatest admiration for the young Mozart, and said so in unmistakable terms.

Many of the names that have just been mentioned mean nothing to a present-day audience. But if one is to understand what these trips with his father meant for Mozart and his development, they must be mentioned if only for their diversity and range. Today we have easy access to the latest musical products from all parts of the world, if we so desire. At Mozart's time few young people received such a comprehensive musical education as he – comprehensive by the standards of his time.

The question arises whether Mozart, for all his gifts, would have become ossified like his father in the traditional musical idiom of his time, if he had spent his childhood solely in Salzburg (and if he had not later been able to tear himself away from that town). In all probability the diversity of the musical experiences he was exposed to on his journeys fostered his inclination to experiment and seek new syntheses of the various schools of his time. It may have made its contribution to his special ability to give free rein to his musical daydreaming while never losing control of it.

It is possible to trace how Mozart first assimilated what he received from others by imitation, in which he was aided by his extraordinary musical memory. Only gradually, as he grew up, was he able to fuse what he had learned with his own fantasies to make something new, something never previously heard. A notebook from the London period shows him at eight and nine still quite clumsily trying to link together the impressions he was receiving. The synthesis, the elaboration of the pre-existing canon into an individual musical language, was a long process demanding much toil and effort, and very largely dependent on the circumstances of his life.

Of course, the opportunity to profit from the wealth of stimuli would have been wasted if the person exposed to them had not had the necessary receptivity. Mozart undoubtedly had this to the highest degree. His early, intensive acquaintance with music, his long, strict training by his father, his stimulating but laborious career as a prodigy in conjunction with his family's hard struggle for financial survival and status, and their resistance against the perpetual threat of downward mobility – all that turned his individual development in a very specific direction far earlier than is the case with many other people. He must have been exposed continuously to musical stimuli, the changing sequences on the violin and the piano, from the first day of his life; he heard his father, his sister and other musicians practising and correcting their mistakes. It is not so very surprising that he early developed an acute sensitivity to tone differences, a highly perceptive musical conscience which, for example, made the impurity of the sound of the trumpet unbearable to him for many years.

All the same, in his very early childhood his interest was not concentrated on music to nearly the same degree as happened later. That old family friend, the trumpeter Schachtner, relates that what struck him especially about the young boy was his total absorption in whatever was occupying him at the time: 'Whatever he was given to learn he applied himself to so totally that he put everything else, even music, aside. For example, when he learned arithmetic the table, the chairs, the walls and even the floor were covered in chalk figures.' And somewhat earlier: 'He was all fire; he was captivated by every subject. I think that in the absence of the exemplary education he received he might have become the most reprobate rascal, so susceptible was he to every stimulus, while not yet able to discern whether it was beneficial or harmful.'[17] Here we have it unequivocally. The small child first displayed an unusual absorption in whatever took hold of his imagination, a susceptibility to stimuli that was not confined to music.

From about his third year Mozart's development became visibly more focused on performing and composing pieces of music. His energies were concentrated at an early stage on specific sublimation processes, on evolving specialised areas of conscience and knowledge that furthered the flow of instinctive fantasies rather than opposing them. That such a timely concentration can be of extreme significance is suggested by a number of observations. The function of this concentration, beginning early and continuing for many years – which is found in simpler societies and in artisan circles more often than in complex industrial societies – in relation to the structure of the personality, the completion and rounding of a gradually developing talent, has been little studied up to now. For this reason, too, it is worthwhile to consider the careers of people who have undergone a one-sided artist-craftsman's education at an early age and have proved extraordinarily gifted and inventive as they grew up.

Moreover, in Mozart's case the researcher has access to extensive, though certainly not complete, contemporary

---

17 *Mozart. Die Dokumente seines Lebens*, pp. 398, 396.

documentation. It indicates very vividly how indissoluble was the link between Mozart's very early artistic specialisation and his wider human development.

At first without realising it, and then more and more consciously, his father guided the child's impulses, and so a good part of his fantasies, into this one channel, the pursuit of music. The intensive training he gave his son included some other things. But music, the training of a virtuoso, was at its centre. The strenuous professional work that was required of Mozart in his childhood and afterwards drove his development in the same direction. And his musical specialisation was, no doubt, also driven by the fact that, for all the deprivations his labours caused him, they also brought intense pleasure and fulfilment.

As a child Mozart cannot have been insensible to the applause, affection, friendship and kindness of the people he met on his concert tours. Empress Maria Theresa, as already mentioned, sent him and his sister elegant, glittering court clothes that had previously belonged to young members of her own family. The seven-year-old ate at the same table as the king and queen of France. The king of England, who drew him affably into conversation after a concert, happened to meet the Mozart family next day as they were out walking in London; driving past them in his carriage, he leant out and waved to the young boy before the whole world. The pope awarded him a distinction that carried the rank of knight, thus doing him an honour for which the great Gluck had to wait much longer (incidentally, Mozart hardly ever used the title). He was feted. Poems were written in his honour. Here is one of them:

To the Six-year-old Pianist from Salzburg
                    Vienna, 25 December 1762...

You admirable child, all praise your skill
And call you both the smallest and the greatest player.
Music for you holds few alarms,

And soon you will be its greatest master.
I only wish your body may withstand your ardent soul,
Not going early to the grave, like Lübeck's child.[18]

This was not the only contemporary voice which expressed anxiety over the dangerous life a prodigy led. Other prodigies had been seen to rise suddenly and brilliantly like fireworks and as quickly be extinguished. In Mozart's case, too, the question arose whether he was a hothouse plant. The suspicion that such a child must have been brought on too quickly and that his talent would not last was hard to avoid and was not unfounded. For the first twenty years of his life Mozart was subjected to a stimulating but extremely severe regime. It is perhaps less surprising that this highly specialised apprenticeship enabled him to perform extraordinary feats in his special field than that it did not cause greater damage to his general development as a human being.

The praise, admiration and gifts he received for the labours he had to perform as a child may have strengthened Mozart's resistance. The deep uncertainty whether he was loved that never left him throughout his life may have been alleviated by the experience of receiving much love in symbolic form for his art. In the course of years his increasing awareness of his value as an artist gave him greater confidence and pride. It is quite conceivable that the reward through this feeling made it easier for him to bear the limitations and burdens of his life as an itinerant prodigy. They may have spurred him to become a master of his craft.

One can understand that with this kind of education and career, Mozart became a highly competent specialist in his field while still a child. The early training by a father who himself had an extremely demanding conscience and corrected all his children's musical mistakes rather severely, gave rise in his son, as often happens, to the formation of a

18 Schenk, *op. cit.*, p. 74.

conscience no less rigorous than his father's, but also quite different in character. The father was a pedagogical perfectionist; he demanded the best from his pupils and from himself as a teacher. The son was a perfectionist as a musician; his artistic conscience, through its fusion and reconciliation with a fantasy-stream purified of all forbidden content, made possible achievements, first as a virtuoso performer and then as a composer, which satisfied his own demand for perfection.

But the unplanned process of development within his family on which this sublimatory aspect of Mozart's musical socialisation was based had no small price. It gave rise to certain peculiarities of his personality that are often regarded as eccentric. This is the point that must be addressed if we are to understand that a person is not an artist in one compartment and a human being in another.

Mozart's Youth – Between Two Social Worlds

Mozart's father, as has been said, was full of contradictions. He saw himself quite genuinely as an enlightened person and yet was an opponent of the Enlightenment. He was plagued by guilt, depression and a despotic conscience and was intellectually, if not as a conductor, highly talented. He took a keen interest in all the political goings-on around him, in all the novel sights he saw on his travels; he had a mental horizon probably a good deal wider than those of most of his colleagues in the Salzburg court orchestra. With this he combined a secret contempt for the dignitaries at the small episcopal court that was obliged, with insufficient means, to ape the pomp of a large court, and therefore to pay for an orchestra of its own, without which a court was unthinkable.

Anyone who wishes to visualise the situation of a gifted commoner in a society dominated by court aristocrats can hardly do better than read the letters of Leopold Mozart. They give a vivid impression of the inescapably subordinate position of bourgeois retainers in this world. Just because Mozart's father had to live at one of the small, rather indigent courts, the constraint which burdened people of his kind was felt by him with particular sharpness. He surely could not entirely conceal his desire to escape these confines

– the trips with his son revealed it. They would not have softened the resentment felt by this or that colleague for someone who seemingly thought himself too good for his station in life.

Nor are his concert tours likely to have made Leopold popular with the dignitaries of the Salzburg court. For them he was a servant, who was expected to behave in accordance with his lowly rank. He had no choice but to conform to this expectation. This is the style in which he had to address his master, the archbishop:

> I now most humbly beg Your Grace not only to pay me for the past month, but as a special favour to give your most gracious order that the sum which has been withheld should also be paid to me. The greater this favour is, the more shall I endeavour to render myself worthy of it and to pray God for Your Grace's welfare.
>
> I and my children send our most humble greetings to Your Grace, our Prince and Lord.
>
>
>
> Your Most obedient
> LEOPOLD MOZART
> Deputy-Kapellmeister[1]
>
>

This letter is dated 8 March 1769. The previous year, the Mozarts had stayed in Vienna to give young Wolfgang the opportunity to demonstrate his virtuosity; as a result, his father's salary had been suspended in April 1768. He himself recognised that this was entirely justified, and it simplified the trip to Italy he was planning at the time. But as he had clearly run into financial difficulties in Vienna, he did finally ask for some back pay. His request was granted to only a minute degree.

Leopold Mozart is in a difficult predicament. The concert tour to Italy with his son is only possible if the income from it exceeds the expenses. Whether that will be the case is in the lap of the gods. On the other hand, he feels that he

1 *LMF*, p. 95.

cannot postpone the journey any longer: 'Or should I perhaps sit down in Salzburg with the empty hope of some better fortune, let Wolfgang grow up, and allow myself and my children to be made fools of until I reach the age which prevents me from travelling and until he attains the age and physical appearance which no longer attract admiration for his merits?'[2]

He was, therefore, only too well aware that as he grew older Mozart's virtuosity would cease to be a special attraction at the courts of Europe. If he was permanently to escape the hated confines of the Salzburg court he had only one chance: to obtain a post for his son at a different, bigger, better situated court. That was the purpose of the trip to Italy, and of the later tours.

Scattered throughout his letters are recurrent references to this plan. Years later Mozart's mother, who was accompanying him on his first tour without his father, wrote from Mannheim: 'I do hope that Wolfgang will make his fortune in Paris quickly, so that you and Nannerl may follow us soon.'[3]

The question is always how to finance the growing prodigy's search for a post, on the success of which the family's happiness, the father's escape from his situation in Salzburg and not least Mozart's own future depend, without sinking into debt. On 15 October 1777 Leopold admonishes his son as follows from Salzburg:

> there you would have the no small advantage of not having to pay anything for food, drink and the rest, in respect of which landlords' bills usually make heavy inroads on one's purse. Now you understand me. *These steps are really necessary and are to your interest.* All the compliments, visits and so forth are only incidental and should not be taken seriously. For you must not lose sight of your main object, which is to make money. All your endeavours should thus be directed to earning money, and you should be very careful *to*

2 Letter of 11 May 1768: *LMF*, p. 85.
3 Postscript to Mozart's letter of 22 February 1778: *LMF*, p. 489.

spend as little as possible, or you will not be able to travel in an honourable fashion, and may even have to remain rooted to one spot and there run up debts.[4]

In retrospect, Leopold Mozart's plan to use his son's special gifts to find an appropriate position for him and a refuge for the family does not seem to have had very great chances of success. At every court there was fierce competition from local musicians for any post that became vacant. Of course, princes and their advisers sought well-known or famous artists from outside for their orchestras, theatres or churches. And concert tours to demonstrate their talents were one of the normal means by which musicians looked out for posts. But precisely what made the young Mozart so admired on his tours, the fact that he was so young, counted against him when it came to finding a permanent post. Leopold Mozart did not, it seems, judge the basic conditions needed for his son's success very realistically.

The members of European court society, particularly the princes, were easily bored. They had obligations that they sometimes fulfilled conscientiously and sometimes did not. But these were not obligations in the sense of professional work. Such work was itself, for them, a characteristic of the lower orders, i.e. the bourgeoisie and the mass of the people. As a leisured class the court aristocracy needed a full programme of entertainments. These included operas and concerts by the musicians employed at court, and performances by travelling virtuosi – or by a child prodigy. Mozart's virtuoso art, above all his power of improvisation, was one attraction among others in the varied programme of entertainments – admittedly a great attraction. Wherever he performed he astonished and delighted his audience by his sensitivity and skill as a pianist, violinist and organist.

The aristocratic members of these court societies lived on inherited income, mainly the yield of an agrarian family estate, or on stipends from court, state or church offices. In

4 *LMF*, p. 320.

such a society what we call art in general, and music in particular, had a different function and therefore a different character to those it has in societies where practically everyone earns a living by regular occupational work. The consensus of the powerful dictated taste in the arts. Music, as has already been discussed, did not exist primarily to express or appeal to personal feelings, the sorrows and joys of individual people. Its primary function was to please the elegant lords and ladies of the ruling class. That does not mean that it had to lack the qualities we refer to by terms such as 'seriousness' and 'depth', but merely that it had to be adapted to the mode of life of the established groups. It was more tightly bound to a social canon, to what we call a style, and the scope for individualisation of the canon was less than is the case with music for working, occupational societies.

There were in court circles many enthusiastic music-lovers. But the broad court public wanted above all to be entertained; they wanted variety. Even Mozart's drawing-power usually waned after a few weeks, the sensation flagged – in Vienna no less than in Naples or Paris. Although individuals here and there continued to show kindness to the prodigy and his family, the great majority of acquaintances quickly lost interest in the performances. An additional difficulty was that on these tours Mozart's father was looking for a post for him. If word of this got about local interests were usually mobilised against him.

Neither the young Mozart nor his father, as far as can be ascertained, had a clear idea of this structural feature of court society. They were never prepared for the fact, and were constantly surprised by it, that the unusual artistry of such a young person was met with growing indifference if they stayed for more than a few weeks at any one place, or visited it a second time after an interval.

One can hardly blame Leopold Mozart for staking everything on one card which, if one looks at it more closely, did not offer much chance of success; for he had no other card to play. With all his might he trained his son for the task of shining before court society first as a virtuoso performer, then as a composer. All other duties and burdens he took from him. He was his son's impresario, responsible for preparing his concerts. He met the costs of the journeys and dealt with the complex problems of currency exchange encountered when crossing the numerous territorial frontiers. Until Mozart finally became independent and married, up to about his twenty-fifth year, practically all his financial affairs passed through his father's hands. This includes the publication of his compositions. On 6 October 1775 Leopold Mozart wrote as follows to J. G. I. Breitkopf in Leipzig: 'As I decided some time ago to have some of my son's compositions printed, I should like you to let me know as soon as possible whether you would like to publish them, that is to say, symphonies, quartets, trios, sonatas for violin and violoncello, even solo sonatas for violin or clavier sonatas.'[5] The publisher thanked him for the kind offer on behalf of his son, but declined in view of the difficult times.

This solicitude may have suited the young Mozart – he was interested only in his music. But his dependence had something double-edged about it. When his father was unable to accompany him on his grand tour of German courts and then to Paris he sent his wife instead, explaining to Wolfgang that he could not be entrusted with money-changing and understood nothing about packing.[6]

A small episode graphically illustrates the relationship between parents and son. Mozart and his mother were about to leave Munich; once again their hopes of a position had come to nothing. There were no openings at the elector's court. Before setting off Mozart writes a long letter to his father. Disappointed about the failure, he asks, among other things, whether he should not seek an opera contract, a *scrittura*, at Naples. He is known there, he argues; an acquaintance has told him that in Naples it is known that no

5 *LMF*, p. 265.
6 II, p. 190.

one plays like Mozart. He is now twenty-one, and in this letter of 11 October 1777 he expresses sentiments characteristic of his affection and his attitude towards his father:

> I can now write the letter to Naples when I choose, but the sooner the better. First, however, I should like to have the opinion of that very wise Court Kapellmeister, Herr von Mozart!
>
> I have an inexpressible longing to write another opera. It is a long way to go, it is true, but it would be a long time before I should have to write it. Many things may happen before then. But I think that I ought to accept it. If in the meantime I fail to secure an appointment, eh bien, then I can fall back on Italy. I shall still have my certain 100 ducats at the carnival and once I have composed for Naples, I shall be in demand everywhere. Moreover, as Papa is well aware, there are also opere buffe here and there in the spring, summer and autumn, which one can write for practice and for something to do. I should not make very much, it is true, but, all the same, it would be something; and they would bring me more honour and credit than if I were to give a hundred concerts in Germany. And I am happier when I have something to compose, for that, after all, is my sole delight and passion. And if I secure an appointment or if I have hopes of settling down somewhere, then the scrittura will be an excellent recommendation, will give me prestige and greatly enhance my value. But all this is only talk – talk out of the fullness of my heart. If Papa can prove conclusively that I am wrong, well, then I shall acquiesce, although unwillingly. For I have only to hear an opera discussed, I have only to sit in a theatre, hear the orchestra tuning their instruments – oh, I am quite beside myself at once.[7]

While Mozart is thus expatiating, his mother is busy with the laborious task of packing. She has just enough time and strength to add a postscript to her son's letter: 'And I am sweating so that the water is pouring down my face, simply from the fag of packing. The devil take all travelling. I feel

---

7 *LMF*, p. 305.

that I could shove my feet into my mug, I am so exhausted. Addio. I kiss you both millions of times . . .'[8]

The image of the mother does not emerge from the sources nearly as clearly as that of the father. Here we get a glimpse of her – a snapshot. Meanwhile the father is sitting impatiently in Salzburg, starting letters before he has had a reply to the last. He suffers, admonishes and warns: 'But by Heaven, if you stayed so long, almost three weeks, in Munich, where you could not hope to make a farthing, you will indeed get on well in this world!'[9] He approves by return his son's idea of writing to Naples. But he can't help adding: 'I myself thought of it long ago.'[10] And again on 15 October: 'What you wrote about the opera in Naples was my idea too.'[11]

We can see the scene before us: the mother packing, the father – worried about the setback and the financial pressure – unable to let go. Only in music does he allow his son any independence. For him, too much depends on the younger man choosing the right path. And he lives in his dreams. His plans cannot be trusted. And when he does suggest something sensible, his father has had the same idea first. He might have denied it, but we can see that in his mind his son was still a child who had to be led in everything, who belonged to him. And his son accepts this. As almost always, he expresses himself very directly and honestly: 'If Papa convinces me that I am wrong, I shall obey.'

The twenty-one-year-old's letter also contains some statements about himself that are to remain true until the end of his life: 'I am happier when I have something to compose', and later: 'I have only to hear an opera discussed . . . to sit in a theatre, hear the orchestra tuning their instruments, – oh, I am quite beside myself at once.' Even by this relatively early age Mozart's whole social existence, with all its passion

8 *LMF*, pp. 307–8.
9 12/13 October 1777: *LMF*, p. 309.
10 *LMF*, p. 310.
11 II, p. 57.

and intensity, has been concentrated on listening to and composing music. He calls it his 'only joy and passion'. This may be somewhat surprising in a young man who also has a lively interest in women and will continue to have in the future. But perhaps he has fewer disappointments in music. Shortly before his death, when his position is desperate, he writes: 'I'm still working, since I find composing less tiring than resting.'[12]

As early as 1777 – as we learn from the same letter – Mozart is already playing with the idea that he is to put into practice some years later. In his disappointment over his failed attempts to gain a fairly secure income through a post at a court, he dreams of the possibility of earning his living by occasional commissions, more or less in the manner of a 'freelance artist' of the nineteenth or twentieth century. In that way, he believes, he can make his reputation. When he has convinced the whole world of his ability by his compositions, especially operas, and his virtuosity, he will not be short of opportunities to earn, whether in the service of a prince or, as we say, on the 'free market'. This idea, and why it was an illusion, deserve further consideration.

Let us picture the actual situation as vividly as possible. Here is a young man with an unusual, almost unique musical gift. All his efforts are directed at realising his talent through composing, and above all by writing operas. Young as he is, he has already produced eight operas, three of which (*Mitridate*, *Ascanio in Alba* and *Lucio Silla*) have been performed in Italy to considerable applause. He knows he can do more and better. That is his desire. But he has to live, to earn money. And when he travels around Europe looking for a post, he comes up against an impenetrable wall, in Vienna, in Munich, in Augsburg, Mannheim, Paris and other places he passes through. The problem clearly is not that the extent of his talent is unrecognised. But that so

---

12 Letter of September 1791 to da Ponte (its authenticity has been questioned); Hildesheimer, *op. cit.*, p. 193.

young a man should aspire to such extraordinary achievements seems, if we read between the lines of his letters, to
frighten off the people responsible for allocating posts.

In his personal demeanour, in his monomaniacal concentration on his art, in his way of dealing with people, Mozart
did not really fit into aristocratic court society. A comparison
with other members of the petty bourgeoisie who success-
fully gained admission to that society makes his difficulties
clearer. Take Rousseau, for example. At an early age he fled
the petty bourgeoisie of Geneva, from which he came. In
France a noblewoman considerably older than him took
him under her protection; she became his mistress and
helped the somewhat rough-hewn young man from French
Switzerland to civilise himself in the court manner. A year
in Venice and the frequenting of financiers' *salons* in Paris
shaped him further in the same direction. In Parisian *salons*
people were prepared to give obvious talent a chance
provided its owner did not bore them and provided he or she
bowed to the canons of feeling and behaviour upheld in
those circles. As a writer Rousseau was one of the first
representatives of an alternative movement directed against
the ruling canon of his society. It is very doubtful that his
works would have been received in court circles if he had
not been personally known there. In social intercourse he
had a certain 'polish'. Without it he would have been
unlikely to have much success with his works, which
advocated a rejection of this polish and extolled the virtues
of a simpler, more 'natural' state of being. Without his
resonance in the Parisian *monde* his works could hardly
have been accepted into the European intellectual tradition
to the extent that was later the case.

Things were different with Mozart. His work was deeply
influenced by the canon of music-making prevalent in the
court and aristocratic society of his time – even though he
extended this canon in a unique manner as he grew older.
But in his demeanour he was nothing less than an *homme
du monde*. He was in the habit of saying outright what he
felt and thought, without much concern for how it would be

received. The habit of holding oneself in reserve in social intercourse to avoid giving offence, the art of everyday diplomacy, the anticipation of the effect produced by one's words and gestures on one's interlocutor that was an inseparable part of social discourse among court people, all this was almost entirely lacking in Mozart. He could conceal himself, he sometimes made use of life's petty lies, but he did not do so very adroitly. He felt most comfortable with people in whose company he could let himself go. In some periods of his development he had an almost compulsive need to say the coarse and obscene things that came into his mind – a need that will be discussed later. Because the art of human intercourse practised and expected in the ruling circles was fundamentally alien and even repugnant to Mozart, he never felt at home in the courtly, aristocratic world. He remained clearly an outsider, nurturing towards this world an increasing antagonism and rebelliousness that manifested itself, for example, in the choice of Beaumarchais's sensational Parisian comedy *The Marriage of Figaro* as the libretto for one of his operas, or in the notably anti-aristocratic *Don Giovanni*.

Leopold Mozart probably had some skill in dealing with his social superiors of the court aristocracy. How far it went, how far he was able to appear as an equal in these circles on his long journeys with his son and daughter, then with his son alone, is difficult to ascertain. His situation was not an easy one. Particularly at the smaller and relatively poorer courts of the German empire it was customary to make social inferiors emphatically aware of their subordinate position, and something of this attitude has perhaps passed into the German tradition. In the Salzburg hierarchy the Mozarts held a relatively low rank, and there were no doubt occasions enough when they were made to feel it. At the bigger courts, however, the aristocrats were often far more conciliatory, and in foreign countries, particularly at the music-loving courts of Italy, the prodigy and his father seem often to have received a heartfelt welcome untroubled by differences of rank. Leopold Mozart, with his whole family, was put in a distinctly awkward position in Salzburg by the triumphs of his son, which were also his own. To avoid these dangers was anything but simple.

The contradiction between the Mozarts' growing fame in the world at large and their lowly position at home can be clearly seen from a little scene the father describes in a letter.[13] Mozart's opera *La finta giardiniera* is performed in Munich. After the premiere the prince-bishop of Salzburg, Count Colloredo, the employer of Leopold and Wolfgang Mozart, comes to the Bavarian court and has the embarrassment of 'hearing the opera praised by the whole family of the Elector and by all the nobles'. Count Colloredo, who is accustomed to treating his deputy conductor and his son very condescendingly as servants, is uneasy at this chorus of congratulation and, as Leopold Mozart describes him, makes an awkward impression. It was, as we can see, a false position which caused resentment on both sides.

While his father may have been able to adapt himself to aristocratic social manners, his son never properly did so throughout his life. It may be easier to understand this trait, too, of Mozart if we bear in mind his strict education, from which he was long unable to protect himself. Something of his protest against his father probably found displaced expression in his rebelliousness towards the dominant order of his time, to which Leopold Mozart more or less submitted.

For many years all Mozart's contacts with other people on his concert tours were arranged by his father and took place under his eyes. If we can rely on the letters, which are our main and often only source, it seems that at about the age of fifteen Mozart underwent a peculiar change, which might be expected at that age but which in many respects took an unexpected course. The restriction of human contacts to those mediated by his father clearly contributed to a certain isolation, an increased dependence on his imagination. On

13   18 January 1775: *LMF*, p. 260.

2 November 1771 he writes from Milan: 'There is a performance of Hasse's opera today, but as Papa is not going out, I cannot be there. Fortunately I know nearly all the arias by heart and so I can see and hear it at home in my head.'[14] Mozart is now almost sixteen. He cannot visit the opera or even leave the house because his father is not doing so. He counters the isolation that this constantly sheltered life brings with it by withdrawing into his musical fantasy. He plays an opera he cannot attend in his mind.

During this stay in Milan he had, above all, written the *serenata teatrale Ascanio in Alba*, which had been performed on 17 October to celebrate the wedding of Archduke Ferdinand. Again and again the question of an appointment was raised – it was probably more important to his father than anything else. But his attempt to use the opera to get his son a position at the court of Milan failed. Naturally, Leopold Mozart could not have suspected that Empress Maria Theresa had expressly warned the archduke against taking such useless people as the young Salzburg composer into his service: 'If it amuses you, of course I will not prevent you. What I say is that you should not burden yourself with useless people . . . It only debases court service if such people travel around the whole world like beggars.'[15]

A year later father and son were back in Milan, this time to take up an offer of a *scrittura* and so to enhance the young master's reputation as an opera composer. Mozart had much work to do on his new opera seria *Lucio Silla*. He was under considerable pressure, and his head was full of music. All other thoughts vanished: 'I still have fourteen numbers to compose and then I shall have finished. But indeed the trio and the duet might well count as four. It is impossible for me to write much, as I have no news and, moreover, I do not know what I am writing, for I can think of nothing but my

14   *MLF*, p. 205.
15   Letter from the empress of 12 December 1771: *Mozart. Die Dokumente seines Lebens*, p. 124.

opera and I am in danger of writing down not words but a whole aria.'[16]

On this trip, too, there seemed to be the chance of a post, this time at the court of Florence. On the day of the premiere of *Lucio Silla* (26 December 1772) Leopold Mozart sent a copy of the score with a letter to Archduke Leopold of Tuscany; early in 1773 he wrote again, presumably because he had not had a reply. The opera was a success with the Milanese public and was repeated several times, but again nothing came of the post. It is difficult to say how deeply the son was affected by the repeated successes of his music and the equally regular setbacks as regards his post.

Lucio Silla was Mozart's last opera for an Italian public. He had had to make a big effort to finish it and probably had a little help from experienced Italian composers; the year before, with *Ascanio in Alba*, he had fared little better. Something of his exertions is felt in the short postscripts he adds to his father's letters to his mother and sister in Salzburg on both journeys. He himself writes almost exclusively to his sister. His messages give the impression that his energies are so totally concentrated on his musical work that the rest of his life is completely empty. He can't think of anything to write home about because he does not really experience anything.

And because he has nothing to say, he invents comic stories, a kind of joke without a point.[17] These come to the fore at about the same time as his predilection for humorously intended faecal expressions. The letters give the impression that, at fourteen, Mozart still enjoyed his life in Italy, especially Naples. But now, one or two years later, when the latency period is over (and no doubt also because of the fruitless search for a post, which may have affected the son primarily through his frustrated father), conflicts from an earlier phase seem to break out again. The stories

16 Letter of 5 December 1772: *LMF*, p. 219.
17 Rather like English shaggy dog stories.

Mozart tells his sister for lack of other news are very characteristic of the half-conscious feeling of emptiness and meaninglessness that has obviously overtaken him. The refrain 'I don't know anything, Father has already said everything' speaks for itself. This is an example from the stay in Milan of 1771:

> Praise and thanks be to God, I too am well. As my work is now finished, I have more time to write letters. But I have nothing to say, for Papa has told you everything already. I have no news except that numbers 35, 59, 60, 61, 62 were drawn in the lottery; and so, if we had taken these numbers we should have won. But as we did not take any tickets, we have neither won nor lost, but we have had our laugh at other people who did.[18]

The adolescent Mozart makes fun of the people who win or lose. The somewhat spectral kind of humour that comes increasingly to the fore in him clearly stands in close relation to the feeling that life is passing him by, that he is unable either to win or to lose because he has not really played.

A year later there is a second example of the same type, which continues to be found in the correspondence. It throws some light on this half-concealed wretchedness, a curious form of the feeling that 'nothing ever really happens':

> That reminds me. Have you heard what happened here? I will tell you. We left Count Firmian's today to go home and when we reached our street, we opened the hall door and what do you think we did? Why, we went in. Farewell my little lung. I kiss you my liver, and remain as always, my stomach, your unworthy frater brother Wolfgang. Please, please, my dear sister, something is biting me. Do come and scratch me.[19]

18   26 October 1771: *LMF*, pp. 203–4.
19   Milan, 18 December 1772: *LMF*, p. 221. The above text was written by Mozart with alternate lines upside down. There is also a drawing which, as far as it can be construed, seems to show a heart with flames and smoke, perhaps indicating the desire to flee home to his sister.

In this period Mozart felt an increasing inclination to play the clown. In the bantering, affectionate letters they exchanged when apart in their youth, his sister Nannerl often addresses him as 'Buffoon'. He calls himself a 'fool' or a 'poor fool'. In fact, Mozart was not ill-suited to the role of clown, the classical harlequin who cuts his capers before the public while grieving in his heart because his wife loves another. In truth, he was a kindred spirit of Petrushka, whose sweetheart the Moor carries off, a kind of *Pierrot Lunaire*.

In trying to form a picture of Mozart, we are immediately struck by the contradictions in his personality. He is the creator of music which in its way is sublime, pure, immaculate. It has an eminently cathartic quality, and seems to rise above all the animal regions of the human being. It clearly bears witness to a highly-developed capacity for sublimation. But at the same time, Mozart was capable of making jokes that, to the ears of later generations, sound extremely coarse. As far as we can see they have a directly sexual reference only in relation to women with whom he slept or wanted to sleep; for the rest they represent a libidinal breaching of verbal taboos surrounding the anal and sometimes the oral zone. Many such examples are to be found in Mozart's letters; especially notorious in this regard are the 'Bäsle-Briefe' – letters to his cousin Bäsle written at twenty-one or twenty-two, which (if one wishes to put it thus) are products of a delayed puberty.[20] Undoubtedly, he did not play the clown only in his letters.

Some recent biographies understand Mozart's propensity for anal jokes, which occurs mainly but not exclusively at a particular period of his life, as an abnormal personal trait.

---

20 It is known that Stefan Zweig, who owned most of these letters, very circumspectly published one of them privately. He sent a copy of the edition to Freud, commenting on the curious 'infantilism' of their author. Cf. Hildesheimer, *op. cit.*, p. 109.

That is to do him less than justice. Today, such clowning is looked down upon among well-bred people, whose sensibilities it offends. But to see it in Mozart's case as a purely personal aberration is to judge the behaviour and feelings of someone who lived at an earlier time as if he were our contemporary, and to overlook the different standards operating at that time.

To a letter of 4 November 1777 to his father, Mozart added, on the envelope, the following postscript concerning the making of targets for a shooting match:

> Gilowski Katherl, fr: v: Gerlisch, h: von Heffner, fr: v: Heffner, fr: v: Schidenhoven, h: Geschwendner, h: Sandner and all who are dead. As for the targets, if it is not too late, this is what I would like. A short man with fair hair, shown bending over and displaying his bare arse. From his mouth come the words: 'Good appetite for the meal'. The other man to be shown booted and spurred with a red cloak and a fine fashionable wig. He must be of medium height and in such a position that he licks the other man's arse. From his mouth come the words: 'Oh, there's nothing to beat it'. So, please. If not this time, another time.[21]

To be sure, these words show the direction of Mozart's fantasies. But the fact that a son can give his father such instructions without a trace of embarrassment, and ask him to produce targets of this kind for what was probably a public shooting match, also shows how wide was the scope for coprophilous fantasies in his social circle. In this society there was less necessity to conceal them from public view, and therefore to repress them from consciousness, than in industrial societies of the twentieth century.

Undoubtedly, individual personality structures also played a part in Mozart's apparently compulsive use of anal (and sometimes oral) words and images. One may suppose that in him infantile conflicts partly connected with hygienic training in infancy resurfaced at puberty. They may also

21 *LMF*, pp. 357–8.

---

have given indirect expression to aggression against his father, and then more broadly against the established order, that was long denied any direct expression.

That aggressive feelings towards the ruling class of his time were present in Mozart, and that they formed a very dominant trait of his personality structure, can be observed throughout the whole of his later career. His pride, his aversion to 'grovelling' that he writes to his father about, are evidence of this. His unwavering refusal to use the noble title granted him by the pope and to emulate Gluck who, on the strength of a lesser papal distinction, called himself the 'Knight von Gluck' throughout his life, is a symptom of this non-identification with the aristocratic establishment. No doubt, this was an ambivalent attitude. As explained earlier, it went hand-in-hand with a strong desire to be acknowledged and accepted as an equal by court-aristocratic circles – though admittedly on the strength of his achievement as a musician, not his title. And as this acknowledgement was withheld even when he made his early attempts to find a post, Mozart must surely have had strongly negative feelings towards the prevailing society. It is not unlikely that such suppressed aggression erupted in his verbal references to animal functions. Taken in the whole context of his life, that would be very understandable.

But when all this has been said we must add at once that a judgement on Mozart's verbal coprophilia would necessarily miss the mark if it applied present-day standards of civilisation, thus implicitly regarding our own canon of sensibility as universal, a canon for the whole of mankind, and not as one that has developed. To do justice to Mozart's tendency, we need to have a clear idea of the civilising process in the course of which the social canon of behaviour and feeling changes in a specific way. In Mozart's society, in the phase of the social civilising process in which he lived, the taboo on the use of the shocking words one finds in his letters was not nearly as strict and harsh as in our day. Unveiled allusions to excretion were part of the normal amusements of convivial life among the young people – and probably the older ones as well – with whom he associated. They were by no means prohibited, or at most so lightly prohibited that the joint flouting of the taboo caused much merriment among the young people of the time.

Two further examples may clarify the difference between the customs of that time and ours. Among Mozart's closest acquaintances at Salzburg was a friend of his sister called Rosalie Joly. She was the daughter of the court pastry cook, and served as a chambermaid at the house of Count Arco; Leopold Mozart mentions her in a letter of 13 August 1763 as 'Miss Rosalia Joli, chambermaid of Her Excellency the Countess of Arco'.[22] The young Mozart was a good friend of hers. They wrote each other occasional verses. One of these poems, which Rosalie Joly wrote for Mozart's name-day and appended to a letter of his father to his wife of 23 October 1777, gives an impression of the standard of sensibility in Mozart's social circle – at least among young people, but also in full view of the older generation.

> Wolfgang my dearest friend, your name-day is today
> And so I wish for you, my very dearest boy
> As much as you could wish, as much as you deserve.
> Happy you'll always be, and not by beetles bit.
> Fortune that showed you here nothing but Fortune's arse
> Be doubly kind to you, in that far distant place.
> That is my heartfelt wish, as truly as I live,
> And were it possible, I'd more than wishes give.
> So tell you mother please, whom I so much revere,
> That I love her always, and often long to see.
> Her kindness may she keep, and her friendship for me,
> As long as she shall have a crack in her behind.
> Stay healthy dearest friend, in joy and merriment
> And play from time to time a little fart-duet.
>
> Rosalie Joly[23]

This reference to the anatomy of Mozart's mother and to a little fart-duet may be particularly offensive to the present

22 I, p. 87.
23 II, p. 80.

canon of feeling. But it was made here quite clearly without the slightest sense of breaking a taboo. It is not a joke which came from a repressed mind.

Another passage from a postscript by Mozart to a letter from his mother to his father of 14 November 1777 makes clear how much verbal 'filth' was an element of convivial behaviour among young and even older people:

> I, Johannes Chrisostomus Amadeus Wolfgangus Sigismundus Mozart hereby plead guilty and confess that yesterday and the day before (not to mention on several other occasions) I did not get home until midnight; and that from ten o'clock until the said hour at Cannabich's house and in the presence and company of the said Cannabich, his wife and daughter, the Treasurer, Ramm and Lang I did frequently, without any difficulty, but quite easily, perpetrate – rhymes, the same being, moreover, sheer garbage, that is, on such subjects as muck, shitting and arse-licking – and that too in thoughts, words – but not in deeds. I should not have behaved so godlessly, however, if our ringleader, known under the name of Lisel [Elisabetha Cannabich], had not egged me on and incited me; at the same time I must admit that I thoroughly enjoyed it. I confess all these sins and transgressions of mine from the bottom of my heart and in the hope of having to confess them very often, I firmly resolve to go on with the sinful life which I have begun. Wherefore I beg for the holy dispensation, if it can be easily obtained; if not, it's all one to me, for the game will go on all the same.[24]

As a young man Mozart knew exactly where such jokes were allowed and where they were not; he knew that they were permitted and appreciated among the lower bourgeois court employees, who included the musicians, and even then only among close acquaintances, but that they were wholly out of place in higher circles.[25] As has been

24 *LMF*, p. 373.
25 In a different context I have analysed this difference as a formality – informality gradient: cf. Norbert Elias, *Studien über die Deutschen. Machtkämpfe*

mentioned, from his childhood on Mozart moved in two social worlds – the non-courtly circle of his parents, which could be referred to today by the somewhat inappropriate term 'petty bourgeois', and the court aristocrats who still felt quite secure in their power in German and Italian regions, despite the distant lightning and the first rumblings of the French Revolution.

The split in his social existence made itself felt in his personality structure as well. Mozart's entire musical activity, his whole training as a virtuoso performer and composer, were shaped by the music canon of the hegemonic court societies of Europe. His work was largely characterised by its attunement to court-aristocratic circles, not merely through the conscious, deliberate adaptation of his works to emperors, kings and other high patrons, but also through the involuntary adjustment of his artistic conscience to their musical tradition. This attachment of his conscience allowed him enough latitude to develop the court tradition in an entirely personal way, without ever breaching its boundaries. But through his individual imagination he carried it in many cases far beyond the understanding of the actual court-aristocratic audience.

At the same time, in his personality structure, especially as far as his social relations were concerned, he remained a man of the petty bourgeoisie – 'petty bourgeoisie' not in our sense but in that of Mozart's time, when people confronted their fellows far more directly as regards liking or disliking. His uncourtly social habitus stood in a paradoxical relationship to his work. And this paradox undoubtedly contributed considerably to his social failure – no less than to the triumphant march of his music after his death.

There seems good reason to suppose that Mozart's relationship to women was conditioned by this existence in two different social worlds. On one hand he lived on the closest

und Habitusentwicklung im 19. und 20. Jahrhundert, ed. by Michael Schröter, Frankfurt am Main 1989, pp. 38–44.

terms with women like his mother, his sister and her girlfriends, for whom coarse jokes involving physical contact – within limits – were among the normal and permitted erotic games of youth. The limits were strict. It is doubtful whether the thought of sleeping together before marriage occurred in the young Mozart's social circle, let alone the practice. When his sister married, Mozart sent her a serious little poem for her wedding, in which he spoke clearly and directly: 'You will now learn much that was half concealed from you before. Things may not always go smoothly. Men are sometimes bad-tempered. But remember: they rule by day, and women by night.'[26]

Apart from this, from an early age Mozart had contact with women of a quite different type, the female members of the court nobility. One cannot avoid asking what would have happened if one of the experienced court ladies had taken him as an adolescent or a young man under her protection and given him access to a liaison that he never attained; that such relationships were quite common is shown by Rousseau's case. But for Mozart there was the double obstacle of supervision by his father and by his conscience. He was always very susceptible to what might be called the aura of femininity. It was said that he fell in love with every one of his female pupils.[27] Many if not most of them came from noble circles, especially during the Viennese period. They were unattainable to him. His longing, his desires in relation to them certainly lay in the direction we call 'erotic'. He dreamed of them, and it is not unlikely that a breath of their elegance and charm sometimes passed into his music, no less than an echo of his melancholy at their unattainability and his indignation over his fate.

His contacts with women from his own class sometimes – perhaps not very frequently – gave rise before his marriage to relationships in which the erotic aspect was surpassed by

26 Letter of 18 August 1784: III, p. 321.
27 Cf. Hildesheimer, *op. cit.*, p. 276.

the sexual element or entirely eclipsed by it. Something of the different roles these two feminine types played in Mozart's life is discernible in the letters he wrote to representatives of both types. I choose as examples a letter to Aloisia Weber, the sister of his future wife, who later became famous as a great opera singer, and another to his cousin, who was probably his first lover:[28]

Dearest friend! I hope that you are in excellent health – I beg you to take great care of it – for good health is the best thing in the world. Thank god, I am very well, as far as my health is concerned, because I watch it. But my mind is not at rest – nor will it be until I have heard (and what a comfort that will be) that your merits have received their just reward. Yet my condition and my situation will be the happiest on that day when I shall have the infinite pleasure of serving you again and embracing you with all my heart. This too is all that I can long for and desire, and my only consolation and my sole comfort lie in this hope and desire . . . Addio, for the present, dearest friend! I am very anxious to get a letter from you. So please do not keep me waiting and do not make me suffer too long. In the hope of having news from you very soon, I kiss your hands, I embrace you with all my heart, and am, and ever shall be, your true and sincere friend

W A MOZART[29]

In the greatest haste . . . I now write to inform you that tomorrow I am leaving for Munich. Dearest coz, don't be a fuz. I would gladly have gone to Augsburg, I assure you, but the Imperial Abbot wouldn't let me go . . . Perhaps I shall take a trip from Munich to Augsburg. But I am not sure about this. So if it really gives you pleasure to see me, come to Munich, that fine town. Make a point of being there before the New Year . . . So come for a bit or else I'll shit. If you do,

28 *Editor's note*: The manuscript breaks off at this point. The two letters quoted here are from a collection of photocopies and hand-copies from Mozart's correspondence assembled by Elias. It contains no other letters to Aloisia Weber. A letter of 13 November 1777 is also copied from the collection of the 'Bäsle-Briefe', but there are several copies of that of 23 December 1778. The extracts were chosen by the editor.

29 30 July 1778: *LMF*, pp. 582–83; original in Italian.

this high and mighty person will think you very kind, will give you a smack behind, will kiss your hands, my dear, shoot off a gun in the rear, embrace you warmly, mind, and wash your front and your behind, pay you all his debts to the uttermost groat, and shoot off one with a rousing note, perhaps even let something drop from his boat.

Adieu, my angel, my sweetheart.

I am aching to see you.

Do send me a nice little letter of 24 pages to Munich, Poste Restante . . .

votre sincere . . . W:A[30]

---

[30]   23 December 1778: *LMF*, pp. 643–4.

PART II

Mozart's Revolt: from Salzburg to Vienna

In May 1781 the tension between Mozart, the disgruntled young musician, and his no less irritated employer and ruler the archbishop of Salzburg, Count Colloredo, became open conflict. It had been a warped relationship from the first, with conflict almost inevitable. Mozart, through his uncommon talent as a performer and composer, had made a name for himself among the music-loving aristocracy at the courts of Europe while still a young man. But in Salzburg itself he occupied a position not formally very different to that of a cook or a manservant. In his own country, therefore, the small absolutist state ruled by Count Colloredo, Mozart was an anomaly.

After the failure of his search for a post at other courts he had returned to serve in Salzburg, since he had no other choice. He had been lucky. The previous court organist had just died, leaving a vacancy. Mozart, or most probably his father on his behalf, immediately applied for the post. In the style of the time (which reveals so unambiguously the enormous power discrepancies in eighteenth-century society) he commended himself to the archbishop 'in deepest subservience to Your Supreme Excellency and Grace'.[1] The

---

1 *Mozart. Die Dokumente seines Lebens*, p. 163.

archbishop himself was very well aware of the prestige it brought to him to have such a famous son of Salzburg as a member of his court. Accordingly, by a decree of 17 January 1779, he ordered the appointment of the young man as court organist, with the same salary, 450 gulden, as his predecessor, an older man and a father of a family.

For a young musician this was not at all bad by the standards of the time, and certainly not ungenerous on the archbishop's side. But the decree of appointment specified in the customary ritual language that the new organist, just like the old one, was to fulfil all his official obligations both in the court chapel and the cathedral, and at court, zealously and unquestioningly – not to mention the compositions that he had to supply at any time for church and court use. By tradition these duties also implied those of a valet de chambre, requiring Mozart to present himself at court each day. His predecessor had clearly accepted these latter duties without complaint, as something self-evident and inescapable. Mozart did not do so, and said later that he had known nothing about such duties. He had merely been advised a few times, he claimed, that he should appear more regularly at court. He had gone only when he was expressly summoned. His negligence in this regard was one of the main reasons why the archbishop was dissatisfied with his services.[2]

In addition, after his reinstatement Mozart was sometimes away from Salzburg for weeks. In autumn 1780 he humbly requested leave of absence as the Bavarian court had asked him for a new opera seria for the carnival festivities of 1781. Mozart needed the vacation to write the opera in great haste and to rehearse it with the singers in Munich. The libretto

---

2 Mozart to his father, 12 May 1781 (*LMF*, p. 730): 'Well, without losing my temper (for my health and my life are very precious to me and I am only sorry when circumstances force me to get angry) I just want to set down the chief accusation which was brought against me in respect of my service. I did not know that I was a valet – and that was the last straw. I ought to have idled away a couple of hours every morning in the antechamber. True, I was often told that I ought to present myself, but I could never remember that this was part of my duty, and I only turned up punctually whenever the Archbishop sent for me.'

– *Idomeneo, Rè di Creta* – which was also to be written by a Salzburg artist, had been prescribed by Munich. (Although he took the liberty of amending the libretto here and there, the craft quality of the whole procedure is still evident: the elector of Bavaria not only gives the composer the commission, but specifies the subject and the text, expecting a new treatment to his own taste.) It was hard for the archbishop to withhold his consent to such a project. It would have looked like discourtesy towards the Bavarian court, which the socially inferior Colloredo could not risk. He therefore held his peace and granted the six-week leave of absence, annoyed as he may have been in secret, for he, after all, was paying Mozart. As I said, a warped relationship.

Mozart for his part was a proud young man who knew his own worth. He had to force himself to adopt the subservient posture demanded of him in Salzburg by the prince and many, if not all, of the court nobles – a posture his father tried to inculcate in him. But now (from the beginning of November 1780) he was in Munich, working on his *Idomeneo.* He loved this kind of work; it absorbed him completely. He outstayed his leave of absence and let events take their course. He would not really have minded if the archbishop had dismissed him. At the Bavarian court he was, to the superficial observer, treated as an equal by the noble lords. As so often he took this at face value, interpreting it as a sign that after the success of his opera he was sure of a permanent post, if not at Munich then somewhere else. He had had enough of Salzburg. By overrunning his leave he was challenging the archbishop. On 16 December he sketched his view of the situation in a letter to his father:

A propos, what about the Archbishop? Next Monday I shall have been away from Salzburg for six weeks. You know, my dear father, that it is only to please you that I am staying on there, since, by Heaven, if I had followed my inclination, before leaving the other day I would have wiped my behind with my last contract, for I swear to you on my honour that

113

it is not Salzburg itself but the Prince and his conceited nobility who become every day more intolerable to me. Thus I should be delighted, were he to send me word in writing that he no longer required my services; for with the great patronage which I now have here, both my present and future position would be sufficiently safeguarded – save for deaths – which no one can guard against, but which are no great misfortune to a man of talent who is single. But I would do anything in the world to please you. Yet it would be less trying to me, if I could occasionally clear out for a short time, just to draw breath. You know how difficult it was to get away this time: and without some very urgent cause, there would not be the slightest chance of such a thing happening again. To think of it is enough to make one weep.[3]

In reality Mozart had little chance of gaining a foothold at the Bavarian court. He was stubborn, where his music was concerned. Sometimes he even crossed swords with the influential theatre director. The high lords were little used to contradiction from subordinates, still less from so young a man. If something in the opera was not to their taste, they said so and expected a suitable change. In their eyes there was no doubt that people of their class who took an interest in the theatre were better judges of good taste than a bourgeois musician. But in matters of music Mozart seldom gave way. He was young, full of dreams and with little knowledge of the world. So they let him have his way. In the end, it wasn't important. But in someone seeking a permanent appointment this insistence on his own ideas was hardly a recommendation.

He therefore stayed in Munich although his leave had run out, and on this occasion his father was fully on his side. He disliked Salzburg no less than his son; but he dared not say so, nor could he afford to. He wrote to his son that Salzburg was full of praise for his new opera, excerpts of which had been performed in advance.[4] As for the extended leave, he

3 *LMF*, p. 690.
4 25 December 1780: III, pp. 69–71.

would simply plead ignorance. If asked by the court, he would reply that they had understood the leave to mean that Mozart could stay in Munich for six weeks after completing the composition as he was needed for the rehearsals and the whole preparation for the performance. Or was His Grace of the opinion that such an opera could be composed, copied out and rehearsed in six weeks? Leopold Mozart knew, of course, that the archbishop's hands were tied. To order Mozart back to Salzburg or to dismiss him while he was working on the Bavarian elector's orders on an opera for his carnival entertainment would have been an affront to the latter. But perhaps Leopold did not allow for the possibility that, although unable to act for the present, the archbishop would become gradually more and more infuriated over the absence of his employee. Mozart's concern was his opera (and the rosy future it seemed to promise), the archbishop's the loss of services for which he was paying, and the disobedience of a subordinate. A naked power-struggle on a petty scale, of the kind that often occurs.

On 13 January 1781 Act III of *Idomeneo* was given its first rehearsal. Friends from Salzburg came to Munich to witness the presentation of Mozart's opera. On 26 January his father and sister arrived. On 27 January, Mozart's twenty-fifth birthday, the dress rehearsal was held, and on the 29th the first performance. It was a great success. Still no word came from the archbishop. He was preoccupied with other matters, above all a serious illness of his father. To visit the sick man he travelled with his court to Vienna. From there Mozart finally received the order, on 12 March, to join his master. He left immediately and was accommodated at the archbishop's residence in accordance with his instructions. There were several scenes, in which Colloredo gave Mozart a dressing down. He clearly wanted to demonstrate to the young man that he was master of his own house, calling him an impudent rascal amid much vituperation.

Of what followed we have only Mozart's account, which may be one-sided. The archbishop, too, may not have been made for such confrontations. He was a withdrawn, somewhat peculiar gentleman who could not bear the sight of blood. Mozart's father had reported on this in a letter to Munich.[5] A short while before, the archbishop had cut his finger while eating. When the blood flowed he stood up, pulled himself together in order not to faint in front of the whole company, went into the next room and fell to the floor. A curious man. At the beginning of May he suddenly ordered Mozart to leave his quarters in the Vienna residence. Mozart took a room with his earlier acquaintances from Mannheim, Frau Cäcilie Weber and her daughters, one of whom, Aloisia, was his first great, and still unforgotten, love. Their father had died in the meantime, and the widow Weber let rooms.

The break between Mozart and his master came on 9 May. Hardly had the evicted musician completed his move than he received an order to take an urgent package to Salzburg with the next post. Mozart, who still had to assemble some funds, went to see the archbishop and apologised for being unable to leave so soon. On the advice of a valet he used the white lie that the mail coach was fully booked. According to Mozart, Count Colloredo called him the most disreputable rascal he knew, claiming that no one served him as badly as he. He advised him to go to Salzburg immediately as he had been ordered, otherwise his salary would be stopped. He himself, claims Mozart, had remained calm although the archbishop had called him a rogue and a scamp. He had merely asked whether his Grace was dissatisfied with him. Thereupon the count had flown into a still greater rage and declared he wanted to have nothing further to do with him. Mozart took advantage of this to reply that they should leave it at that; he would tender his resignation the next day.

The archbishop was apparently unprepared for this. He wanted to impose obedience on Mozart, but hardly expected his subordinate to add fuel to the fire and quit his service. From the archbishop's standpoint the young man's reaction

5   30 December 1780: III, p. 75.

was quite irrational. He had scoured the country for a post and found nothing until the Salzburg court graciously received him back, and with an increased salary. But Mozart was firmly resolved to stay in Vienna. On 9 May, immediately after the row with the archbishop and still in the heat of anger, he sat down in his new quarters at Frau Weber's to write to his father about these latest events. He told how Count Colloredo had berated him and, with assurances of his love for his father and sister, stressed that he was finished with Salzburg.[6]

Now the little world was really in turmoil. On 10 May Mozart went to see his immediate superior, the head kitchener Count Arco, and handed him a formal letter requesting the archbishop to release him. At the same time he tried to return the money that he had already received for the return journey to Salzburg. In both cases Count Arco refused to accept. He tried, probably in collusion with the archbishop, to dissuade the young man from doing what he planned. He told Mozart that he could not resign his post without his father's consent – that was his duty and obligation. Mozart retorted that he well knew what his duty to his father was. To distract his thoughts he went to the opera that evening, but he was still extremely agitated, shivering with his whole body; he had to leave the theatre in the middle of Act I. The next day he still felt ill; he stayed in bed and drank tamarind water to calm himself.

On 12 May Mozart again wrote to his father, repeating that he was absolutely resolved to leave his post for ever. After the archbishop had humiliated him and besmirched his honour in that way he had no choice. If his father loved his son, he would do best not to express an opinion on the matter.[7]

Some hours later he had clearly composed himself somewhat and sent a second letter. He now tried to

6   III, pp. 110–12.
7   III, pp. 112–14. Second letter: III, pp. 114f.

demonstrate that even on sober consideration his decision was entirely rational. The grave insult he had received was only the last straw. Salzburg offered nothing but confinement – both stimulus and appreciation were lacking. In Vienna he already had many good and useful connections. People invited him, showed him every respect and paid him into the bargain. His father should not worry, even about his own position. The archbishop surely could not be so mean as to take away his father's post because he had fallen out with his son.

Leopold Mozart had his doubts. For him the situation was really extremely precarious and he acted, as so often before, with extreme caution, but also with a certain lack of straightforwardness. It is still difficult to determine whether his actions were guided more by concern for his son's future or for his own. At any rate, he insisted that Wolfgang's honour required that the matter be settled not in Vienna but in Salzburg. Mozart was to come home; that was absolutely necessary if he was to extricate himself from the matter with dignity. He also suspected his son of wishing to stay in Vienna mainly for his pleasure. The renewed link with the Weber family as a lodger clearly filled him with deep distrust – not without reason, as it was soon to transpire. That Mozart had fallen head over heels in love with one of the daughters of this family in Mannheim still weighed on his mind. He knew that there were still two other daughters on the scene, feared the worst and used his full authority to bring his son back to Salzburg. But in all this he must have also feared that the slightest sign of encouraging his son in his disobedience and his plan to resign would be ill rewarded by the archbishop. He therefore wrote straight away to Count Arco to assure him that he in no way approved his son's conduct and that he had demanded his immediate return to Salzburg. He wrote to the same effect to his son.

His father's letter made a deep impression on Mozart. But now that his revolt against the archbishop threatened to widen into a revolt against his father, it suddenly became clear how independent and self-confident he already was in his decisions at that time. He saw quite clearly that in the narrow world of Salzburg there would be no fulfilment for him or his work. Unlike his father he realised that the petty tensions and irritations he was caught up in at the Salzburg court, the humiliations and drudgery he was exposed to there, would be repeated endlessly if he was weak enough to go back.

On the other hand, what he did not see clearly enough, unlike his father, were the difficulties he would face after severing himself from Salzburg. Count Arco, to whom he had handed a second, then a third request for dismissal after the refusal of the first, explained to him very clearly on the last occasion what awaited a young musician who tried to make his way in Vienna without a firm appointment. He told Mozart (who passes it on in a letter to his father): 'Believe me, you allow yourself to be far too easily dazzled in Vienna. A man's reputation here lasts a very short time. At first, it is true, you are overwhelmend with praises and make a great deal of money into the bargain – but how long does that last? After a few months the Viennese want something new.'[8]

This conversation took place at the beginning of June. As can be seen, the dispute between Mozart and his master dragged on for some time. The archbishop was not willing to accept his servant's resignation. Mozart, no less stubborn, submitted one request after another, through the intermediary of the head kitchener. It appears that Count Arco refused to pass them on. To bring the young man to his senses, he went so far as to declare that he too had to put up with cross words from the archbishop. Mozart replied with a shrug: 'You no doubt have your reasons for putting up with it, and I – have my reasons for refusing to do so.'[9]

But the tug-of-war was not yet over, Mozart's resignation still not accepted. Viennese society gossiped about the

8   2 June 1781: *LMF*, p. 739.
9   *Ibid.*

amusing saga. Supporters of both parties exchanged arguments. The archbishop called Mozart an arrogant person. Mozart replied that when he was treated arrogantly he became arrogant himself. The decision came a few days later, about 8 or 9 June 1781. Mozart went once more to Count Arco. When he insisted once again on acceptance of his resignation from the archbishop's service, the count finally lost his patience and kicked the pigheaded young man out of the room.

Mozart was furious. At the same time he clearly felt a certain satisfaction that things had gone so far. Now he could claim with some justice that the Salzburg court had thrown him out. He now had a chance to stay in Vienna. Perhaps he did not find a kick in the pants too high a price to pay. But the repeated abuse from the archbishop and his noble courtiers had, of course, put the self-control of the proud young man to a severe test.

During his career as an infant prodigy Mozart had understandably developed a very strong sense of his own value and of his task as a composer and performer.[10] This assorted ill with his social position as a subordinate and servant. One can understand that for him it was simply not possible to give way and slink back to Salzburg like a whipped dog. He would have lost his health and his inner contentment there, he writes in his first letter of 12 May 1781. Even if he had had to beg, he would have left after that insult – 'For who will let himself be bullied?'[11] However, the great majority of Salzburg subjects had no choice in the matter. Like every 'genius' Mozart was a deviation from the norm in his

---

10 His youth clearly obstructed recognition of this value on many occasions. On 31 October 1777 Mozart writes to his father about his first visit to a rehearsal of the Mannheim orchestra (*LMF*, p. 350): 'I thought I should not be able to keep myself from laughing when I was introduced to the people there. Some who knew me by repute were very polite and fearfully respectful; others, however, who had never heard of me, stared at me wide-eyed, and certainly in a rather sneering manner. They probably think that because I am little and young, nothing great or mature can come out of me; but they will soon see.'

11 12 May 1781 (second letter): *LMF*, p. 732.

society, an anomaly, and one with a somewhat inflammable sense of justice.

Even at the moment of rupture he had had a presentiment of the trouble that a life in Vienna without a firm appointment would bring. But he never ceased to hope that the emperor (or at least a king of similar status) would sooner or later reward a talent like his with a permanent post; and he possessed the inner certainty, born of self-belief, that in the meantime he would find ways and means of keeping himself above water. At twenty-five he had clearly acquired the ability to decide on the path in life that seemed best suited to his needs and talents. And he had the strength to impose this decision on everyone, even his father.

How self-confident he had become is seen in every line of his letters of that time to his father, who tried with all the powers of intelligent argument he could muster to deter him from a step which he regarded as a dreadful mistake. Leopold naturally accused Mozart of forgetting his duty to his prince and his father. But the younger man had already escaped his grasp. Mozart's rebuff was in no way less trenchant than his father's arguments; and it was all the more effective in that it did not outwardly violate the traditional norms of a father–son relationship. Mozart parried the admonitory appeals to filial duty by recalling the duties of a father. On 19 May 1781, for example, he wrote: 'I have not yet recovered from my astonishment and shall never be able to do so, if you continue to think and to write as you do. I must confess that there is not a single touch in your letter by which I recognise my father! I see a father, indeed, but not that most beloved and most loving father, who cares for his own honour and for that of his children – in short, not *my* father.'[12]

By his decision he had to an extent jeopardised his father's position at the Salzburg court. He tried to soothe his worries. But as was his way, in this too he was carried away

12 *LMF*, pp. 733–4.

---

by his imagination. If the worst came to the worst, he declared, his father and sister should just come to him in Vienna; he would be sure to be able to provide for all of them.[13] One can see the magnitude of his dilemma. Up to then the Mozart family had always stuck together in the struggle for survival. The father had always unconditionally helped his son's cause – though no doubt his own at the same time. And the son was deeply attached to his father. However much his love may have been mingled with hostility, the intensity of the letters he wrote to him at that time bears witness to the strength of the bond. Leopold Mozart, however, could not hide from himself that his son was in the process of shattering the family as a survival unit and, despite all protestations to the contrary, of going his own way. He saw much more clearly how slight were the chances that Mozart would be able to earn his living without a permanent post, not to speak of supporting his father and sister. All he knew was that his son was staking everything for which he himself had worked for so long on a single throw of the dice.

Mozart's breaking away from his father was, on closer consideration, an astonishing act. It is essential to pay some attention to this aspect of his maturing, his personal civilising process, if one is to make it clear to oneself and others that the development of the artist is the development of the man. Music specialists may understand much about music and little about human beings, and thus construct an autonomous artist puppet, an immanently developing 'genius'. But in so doing they merely contribute to a false understanding of music itself.

For almost twenty years Mozart had lived with his father. For all that time his father had guided him. For the major part of this impressionable phase he was Mozart's teacher, manager, friend, doctor, travel guide and middle-man in his dealings with other people. We sometimes hear of the childish traits which Mozart retained until his death. He did

---

13   13 May 1781: III, p. 119.

indeed have such traits. Given the long reliance on his father that restricted his chance of independence to music-making and composing, that is hardly surprising.

Mozart was a perceptive observer of what went on around him – with regard to particularities and small matters. But his grasp of reality was limited, and was considerably impaired by wishes and fantasies. When he came to a new court and a prince addressed friendly words to him or one of his works was received with applause, he was seized again and again by the absolute certainty that his dream of a secure position laden with honours was about to be fulfilled. That remained the case almost throughout his life. Only very late, under the growing weight of his debts, did he realise somewhat more clearly that this hope might be an illusion, and this reality–shock did much to break him. His indifference and incompetence in the use of money was no doubt also a residue of his childhood, in which his strong, businesslike father had taken care of all such things for him. Possibly, his spontaneity in turning his fantasies into sounds, his feelings into music, and thus the richness of his musical imagination, was also a residue of childhood – and who would wish this spontaneity of an earlier phase to have been replaced by the lack of spontaneity normal in adults of his society?[14]

But in talking about Mozart's 'childish' traits it is easy to forget how grown-up he was in other respects. Evidence of this is the determination with which he carried through his personal revolt against his employer and ruler, and further evidence is the probably far more difficult revolt against his father. The crisis of this separation, the sign of Mozart's coming of age, may seem like a normal part of the human life cycle. But in view of the depth and length of the preceding bond, the break with the father is nothing less

---

14 However, that his fantasies and feelings, and the passions that fed them, did not run away with him, that he was able to give their energy fresh and pristine expression in musical forms and thereby harness them, is an indication of adulthood – of successful sublimation.

than astonishing. It demonstrates a strength of character which surprises us in view of his education.

Mozart was very anxious, as can be seen from his letters, to have his father on his side. The step he had taken gave a new direction to his whole future – of that he was well aware. And he had taken it without seeking his father's advice. That was something new in his life. He had acted impulsively, but at the same time he realised clearly that he had to act thus and not otherwise.

It is certain that Mozart was able to withstand the combined forces of his ruler and employer and his father only because he was strengthened by his knowledge of the value of his artistic work, and thus of his own worth. This knowledge had been consolidated during the prodigy's long years of travel and apprenticeship, and had clearly not lost one whit of its conviction through the setbacks he suffered in his search for a post.

One cannot avoid asking what would have become of Mozart if he had not been so deeply convinced at a relatively young age of the special nature of his musical gift, and of his duty to devote his life to it – a duty that gave meaning to his existence. Would he have been able to produce the musical works to which he owes his later classification as a genius if in the critical situation of 1781 he had not had the strength to resist the pressure of his ruler, his court superiors and his father – in short, the combined forces of Salzburg? Would we have operas like the *Seraglio*, *Don Giovanni* or *The Marriage of Figaro*, piano concertos like the admirable Vienna series, if he had gone back to serve in Salzburg – with all that meant in terms of instructions from the archbishop – and had not participated, or only sporadically, in the rich musical life of Vienna with its (comparatively) enlightened public? We cannot expect an incontrovertible answer to these questions. But it is very probable that if Mozart had decided, for the sake of earning a living, to obey the archbishop's command and use most of his working energy in the way his employer desired, he would have been more bound by the traditional forms of music-making and would have had less scope to develop the court tradition of music in the way that is characteristic of the works of his Vienna period and of his subsequent fame as a genius.

Mozart did not formulate it in general terms, but what he said and did in this critical period indicates how strongly he felt that he would not achieve fulfilment if he did not have the freedom to follow the musical fantasies that rose up in him – frequently without his bidding. He wanted to write music as his inner voices dictated, not as he was commanded by a person who offended his honour and lowered his sense of his own worth. That was the core of his dispute with the archbishop: a conflict over his personal and especially his artistic integrity and autonomy.

The conflict had been slowly brewing and burst out for the first time in the unequal struggle with his princely master and then in his emancipation from his father's guidance. From now on – with shorter and longer breaks – Mozart was pursued by it, just as in ancient mythology someone was pursued by the Furies. Only there it was the compulsion of a fate determined by the gods that drove people guiltlessly guilty into conflict. Here it was quite nakedly a compulsion arising from the co-existence of people and their unequal power-potentials – a social conflict – that was involved. It was fought out first between a ruling prince and an employee who possessed unusual talent and wished to follow his own voices, his own artistic conscience, his own sense of the immanent rightness of sequences of notes that arose in him as words do in others. But at the same time more was at stake than merely two people: two different conceptions of the social function of the musician, one of which was firmly established while the other had as yet no proper place. It was therefore also a conflict between two kinds of music, one of which, the craft music of the court, corresponded to the prevailing social order while the other, that of the freelance artist, was in contradiction to it.

The position of the musician in this society was basically that of a servant or official craftsman. It was not very different to that of a wood-carver, painter, cook or jeweller who, at the behest of fine ladies and gentlemen, had to produce tasteful, elegant or even mildly stimulating products for their edification and entertainment, to enhance the quality of their lives. Mozart undoubtedly knew that his art, as he saw it, would wither if he had to produce music to the orders of uncongenial, indeed hated people whom it would please, regardless of his own mood or his inner affinity to what was demanded. Despite his youth he felt very clearly that his energy as a composer would go to waste if it consumed itself in the narrow confines of the Salzburg court and the tasks it set, particularly as there was not even an opera house and only a mediocre orchestra. The archbishop for his part was doubtless aware that the young Mozart was uncommonly talented and that it would increase the prestige of his court to have such a man among his servants. He was also prepared to lend him to other courts if need be. But in the end he expected Mozart to fulfil his duties and, like any other artisan or servant, to deliver what he was paid for. In short, he wanted Mozart to produce divertimenti, marches, church sonatas, masses or any other fashionable piece of the time, whenever it was needed.

That, then, was the conflict – a conflict between two people, certainly, but two people whose relationship to each other was shaped to a very high degree by their difference in rank and thus in the means of power at their disposal. It was within this constellation that Mozart took his decision. One must bear the inbuilt power difference in mind to appreciate how strong were the forces that drove him to take it.

To recall that Mozart once stood at such a crossroads, that he was forced to take a decision affecting the whole further course of his life – and not least to recall that he took it one way and not another – is to be made more clearly aware how mistaken is the conceptual severance of the 'artist' from the 'man'. We see here most clearly that Mozart's musical development, the special quality of his evolution as a composer, is inseparable from the development of other aspects of his person – in this case, for example, his ability to recognise which career, indeed which geographical location, would be most fruitful for the unfolding of his talents. The idea that 'artistic genius' can manifest itself in a social vacuum, regardless of how the 'genius' fares as a human being among others, may seem convincing as long as the discussion remains at a very general level. But if we examine exemplary cases with all the relevant detail, the notion of an artist developing autonomously within a human being loses much of its plausibility.

Mozart's revolt against prince and father is such an exemplary case. It is not difficult to imagine what the mood of the twenty-five-year-old would have been if he had prevailed upon himself to obey his master's command and return to his native city. Many musicians of his time and his age would probably have done so. Mozart would then, in all probability, have lived in Salzburg like a bird with clipped wings. The necessity of deciding thus would have affected him at the core of his courage to face life, and of his creative power. It would have robbed him of the feeling that he could have a fulfilling task, that his life could have a meaning.

All the same, in the social conditions of the time and for a musician of his rank it was a highly unusual decision that Mozart took. A generation earlier it would probably have been unthinkable for a court musician to give up a post without having found another. At that time practically no alternative was in sight within this social space. On his visit to Vienna Mozart had looked around, partly with the help of families he knew among the court aristocracy, for alternative means of earning. The hopes this had aroused played a major part in his decision to resign his post in Salzburg. He was able to entertain his desire for personal fulfilment and to settle as a kind of 'freelance artist' in

Vienna because conditions in the Austrian capital had developed to a point where they offered him a slight chance of survival.

Whether his decision was realistic is a different question. Perhaps the older people were right who warned of the extreme insecurity of life in Vienna as a musician without a firm post and a fixed salary, and regarded his decision as a sign of his youthful folly, his ignorance of the world. At that time, and even today, it seldom happens that a person's striving for meaning and fulfilment, and the quest for a secure existence, point in the same direction. However, Mozart himself probably had little doubt as to how he should decide. In his eyes the return to Salzburg would have emptied his life of meaning; for him the plan of breaking with Salzburg and staying in Vienna made perfect sense. In Vienna he could breathe more freely, even if it cost him considerable effort to earn his living. Here he had no master with the right to order him about.

Of course, he was still dependent on other people. But it was a somewhat looser (and less secure) dependence. Even while he was living at the archbishop's residence and had had to bend himself to the servant's role along with a host of other house musicians, he had revived his earlier contacts with the Viennese court aristocracy. Countess Wilhelmine Thun, the court and state chancellor Count von Cobenzl, had invited the unusually gifted young man to visit them. He had started looking for piano pupils, apparently with some success. As early as May 1781, before the kick that sealed his departure from Salzburg, he had told his father about a 'subscription for six sonatas'.[15] He was referring to some pieces for piano and violin that he dedicated to a pupil, Josepha von Auernhammer, and which appeared in print at the end of November the same year. Vienna delighted and stimulated him. For a time after the break with the archbishop he

15   19 May 1781: III, p. 118.

was clearly in very good spirits. As always, he saw the possibility of a congenial post round the next corner; as always, it proved a castle in the air. However, there were as many piano pupils as he could have wanted. But he did not really like teaching and tried to limit it. He was counting on extra income from concerts in nobles' houses, from public subscription concerts and from subscriptions for the scores of his compositions.

And above all, a commission for an opera, with imperial backing, was in the offing. On 30 July 1781 a skilled and experienced author of opera texts, the younger G. Stephanie, gave Mozart the libretto for a German Singspiel with a Turkish subject, *Bellmont and Constance* or *The Abduction from the Seraglio*. Mozart worked on this project with great energy. Something of the joyful liberation of his first Viennese time is felt in the music he wrote for it. More than in his previous operas he took the liberty of developing the court music tradition in which he had grown up, and which had become second nature to him, in his personal way. To be able to do this, more than was permitted in Salzburg – to follow his own musical imagination, was one of his primordial desires. It was, as we have said, his way to fulfilment.

To this extent Mozart did indeed now resemble a freelance artist. But even this early attempt to give free rein to his musical imagination revealed something of the dilemma facing the 'free' artist. In giving latitude to his individual fantasy, and especially to his ability to synthesise previously separate elements in a way which breaches the existing canon of taste, he initially reduces his chances of finding resonance in the public. This need not be dangerous if the power relationships in his society are such that the art-loving public which pays to enjoy art is relatively uncertain in its taste, or at least is dependent in forming its taste on specialised art establishments to which the leading artists themselves belong. It is different in a society whose establishment regards good taste in the arts as in dress, furniture and houses as the natural prerogative of its own social group.[16] Here, a 'freelance artist's' inclination to innovate beyond the existing canon can be extremely dangerous for him or her. Emperor Joseph II, who had involved himself somewhat in the planning of Mozart's opera *The Abduction from the Seraglio* as the prototype of a German Singspiel, was clearly not quite satisfied with the finished work. He told the composer after the Vienna *première*: 'Too many notes, my dear Mozart, too many notes.'

One of the singers, too, seems to have complained that her voice could not be heard above the orchestra. In this respect, too, without realising it, Mozart had inaugurated another shift in the balance of power. At the court opera houses of the old style the singers were in control. The instrumental music was subservient; it was there to accompany them. But in the *Seraglio* Mozart had changed this power balance somewhat; he sometimes liked to intertwine the human and instrumental voices in a kind of dialogue. He thereby undermined the privileged position of the singers. And at the same time he unsettled court society, which was used in an opera to empathising with the human voices and not with simultaneous orchestral voices. If Mozart gave the orchestra something to say, the public did not hear it. They only heard 'too many notes'.[17]

16 In a letter of 4 November 1777 (II, p. 101) Mozart says he has written a concerto for the oboist of the Mannheim orchestra, who was 'mad with joy' about it. When he played the concerto on the piano in the room of the Mannheim conductor the listeners liked it very much. No one, Mozart adds ironically and not without bitterness, said that it was not well composed; but they ought to have asked the archbishop, he would soon have put them right.

This side of Mozart's relationship to his employer needs to be considered if one is to judge its outcome properly. To a member of the ruling class there was no question but that he had the necessary competence to judge on matters of music. And if a servant was as proud of his ability as Mozart, he had to be shown that as a prince one always understood music better than a subject.

17 *Editor's note*: At this point there is a break in the original manuscript; the section which follows is headed Part 2 of 'Act IV' of the drama of Mozart's life ('Mozart in Vienna') and remains a fragment.

Emancipation Completed: Mozart's Marriage

The events described so far, the break with the archbishop, Mozart's decision to leave his native city and live in Vienna as a freelance artist, were only the first steps on the way to detaching himself from his father. The next emancipatory step was Mozart's decision to marry.

One might think that as shrewd a father as Leopold Mozart would have received the news that his twenty-five-year-old son wanted to marry calmly, if not joyfully, as something long expected. Mozart's father was unable to do so, for understandable reasons. He, too, hated the service at the Salzburg court. As deputy conductor he was not particularly well paid, held a relatively low rank quite out of keeping with his intellectual qualities, and was often enough subjected to humiliating treatment. But unlike Mozart he bowed to the inevitable; he accepted the humiliation with gritted teeth and bent his knee. His only chance of escaping the intolerable situation was an elevated, well-paid position for his son. He had always dreamed – like his wife, up to her death in Paris – that he would follow him; and during his years of travel and apprenticeship Mozart, who was financially dependent on his father, had never ceased to nourish these hopes. In the family circle it was taken for granted that they would stay together when the young man had finally found his great position.

Now Mozart was twenty-five, and when he left Salzburg he involuntarily clung to this familiar idea. In his efforts to calm his anxious father he wrote that he would give him half his income as soon as he had a permanent post.[1] He had promised his sister to fetch her and her secret fiancé from Salzburg where – for unknown reasons – it was not possible for them to marry.[2] Behind Leopold's bitter reproaches to his son over his decision in favour of Vienna, and his desperate efforts to make him change his mind, was the fear of the prisoner who sees his hopes of escape vanishing for ever. Most of his letters of that time have been lost. But a reflection of the anxious concern with which he tried to supervise his son's activities from a distance is discernible in the latter's replies.

In this small, relatively confined world letters quickly took Viennese gossip to Salzburg, and the echo of Salzburg gossip back to Vienna. Shaken by the growing independence of his son, on whose fortunes his own future now depended, Leopold clearly kept asking himself: 'What's the boy really up to in Vienna?' He constantly heard rumours that made him uneasy, and straight away sent questions and worried admonitions to his son. It had come to his ears, he wrote, that Mozart was eating meat on meatless days and even boasting about it. Did he not think at all about the salvation of his soul? And his son wrote back at length to say that he had not boasted that he ate meat on fast-days, but had merely said he did not regard it as a sin. He had heard, wrote the father, that Mozart had been seen in the company of a person of ill repute at the carnival ball. And his son replied with his peculiar artful honesty, which concealed much, that he had known the woman in question for a long time before noticing that she did not have a good reputation, and as one needed a partner for the carnival ball it would not have been

1 Letter of 15 December 1781: III, p. 182.
2 19 September 1781: III, pp. 158f.

proper to break off the relationship abruptly, though he had gradually started dancing with others as well.[3]

Then there was the matter of his lodgings. It caused Leopold the most unease. Mozart had taken rooms with the widow Weber and her daughters, whom he knew from Mannheim. One of the daughters who had now married and become a famous singer, he had loved especially – with a great love. He wrote to his father quite openly that his feelings for her were still very much alive. Not that that meant anything, he added, as she was no longer free.[4] But now Mozart was living with Mother Weber and her unmarried daughters like the cock of the walk, and his father was deeply disturbed. Might this not lead to something? So he advised his son with increasing urgency to find other lodgings. He had heard disquieting reports of widow Weber's character. She was a domineering woman who was determined to find husbands for her daughters by any means – including letting rooms. Mozart replied that he would look for other lodgings; in any case, he had other things on his mind than marriage; it was difficult enough to keep himself above water.[5]

The correspondence was not limited to paternal fears about his son's love life or filial attempts to allay them. Mozart told about the opera he was working on. It fully absorbed him – how could he think of marriage? But the librettist, Herr Stephanie, was not supplying the text quickly enough: 'I am beginning to lose patience at not being able to go on writing my opera. True, I am composing other things in the meantime – yet – all my enthusiasm is for my opera, and what would at other times require fourteen days to write I could now do in four.'[6] They also carried on an expert discussion of the opera. Leopold opined that the words Stephanie had put into Osmin's mouth were too coarse, and not particularly good as verse, and his son

---

3 13 June 1781: III, p. 129.
4 16 May 1781: III, pp. 116f.
5 25 July 1781: III, p. 140.
6 6 October 1781: *LMF*, p. 771.

replied that while that was correct it made the poetry suit the character of Osmin, who was a stupid, coarse, malicious fellow. The very roughness of the verse fitted the musical ideas that had already been 'walking about' in his head.[7] Mozart was clearly pleased with the text; it inspired him, conforming to his idea that in an opera the poetry should be in the service of the music. That was why the Italian comic operas got so much applause – in them the music ruled the words.

Undoubtedly, Mozart was not living like a hermit. He liked women, and in Vienna he must have met more women who were to his liking than in Salzburg, while they in turn liked the not very prepossessing but lively, intelligent and unbelievably gifted young musician. We do not know how far these affairs went. But it may be worth mentioning one of them, which wound its way like a little comic thread through the dramatic events of that time.

Among the Viennese ladies of the higher classes who took an interest in Mozart there was, above all, the Baroness von Waldstätten. She had separated from her husband and had a reputation as a somewhat easygoing lady. As far as can be made out, Mozart's relationship with her, of whatever kind it might have been, was the only one that followed the familiar pattern of a liaison between an experienced older woman and a relatively inexperienced young man. Baroness von Waldstätten, *née* von Schäfer, was born in 1741, and so was fifteen years older than Mozart. An attractive forty-year-old when the composer met her, for a time she was mother, friend and patron to him at once. On 3 November 1781 he told his father, not without pride,[8] that on his name–day, after going to early mass and being just on the point of writing to him, he had been visited by a group of well-wishers. At midday he drove to Baroness Waldstätten's in Leopoldstadt, where he spent the day. At 11 at night, just as he was getting undressed to go to bed, six musicians took up

---

7   13 October 1781: III, p. 167.
8   III, p. 171.

their positions in the courtyard and played him a little *Nachtmusik*, his own wind serenade in E flat major (K 375). One can picture the scene, which might have come from one of Mozart's operas, as he listens from the balcony to the musicians clearly sent by the Baroness, thanks them and withdraws.

Soon afterwards, on 15 December, he informed his father that he had decided to marry one of the Weber daughters, Constanze, and asked for his understanding and approval. He admitted that he had hesitated to write the letter, as he could foresee the response. His father was sure to ask how a man without a secure income could think of marrying. But he had very good reasons for taking this step: the voice of nature spoke just as loudly in him as in others – and, he added, 'louder, perhaps, than in many a big strong lout of a fellow'.[9] On the other hand, it was not in his nature to consort with whores or to seduce young girls. He loved Constanze as she did him, and as he needed something certain in love, marriage for him was the only answer.

For his father this decision meant the end of all his hopes. He tried to persuade him to change his mind; he threatened and refused his agreement – as can be read in any biography of Mozart. In the end it was Baroness Waldstätten who got the couple married. Leopold Mozart never quite recovered from this blow.[10]

---

9 *LMF*, p. 783.
10 Particularly as he disliked Constanze as his son's bride and wife. When Mozart married her she was an uneducated young girl who could be very lively and flirtatious when among her close friends. Her attempts to win over Mozart's angry relations, particularly his sister, in postscripts to his letters, show an almost unbearable affectation (admittedly in a difficult situation) that probably had the opposite effect to the one desired. All the more surprising are the measured, well-informed and entirely unaffected letters she wrote in old age, when twice widowed.

The Drama of Mozart's Life:
a Chronology in Note Form

The sociological problem: the transition from craftsmen's art to artists' art

Craftsmen's art (with its offshoots as *court* or *official* art): art production for a personally known patron of far higher social status than the producer (steep power gradient). Subordination of the art producer's imagination to the patrons' canon of taste. Art not specialised, but a function of other social activities of the consumers (primarily an aspect of competitive spending on status). Strong social and weak individual character of art products symbolised by what we call 'style'.

Artists' art: art created for a market of anonymous buyers mediated by agencies such as art dealers, music publishers, impresarios etc. Change in the balance of power in favour of the art producers, assuming they can induce public consensus on their talent. Greater independence of artists from society's artistic taste, social parity between artist and art buyer (democratisation).

Problem: *What are the reasons for the change in the social situation of artists?* Social ascent of mass professional classes; the art buyers are predominantly wealthy members of the middle class or state or civic authorities. It is still an exception for a trade union, e.g. in England, to buy art works systematically as investments.

What changes in artistic form are explained by this change in the social situation of artists? Greater individualisation of the work of art, greater scope for individual artistic fantasy, greater scope for going off the rails, hence increase in kitsch, as the strict canon of artistic taste of a higher social class has largely lost its function as a supervising restraint on individual artistic imagination. The transition from craftsmen's to artists' art is therefore characteristic of a *civilising shift*: greater dependence of the art producer on personal self-restraint in controlling and channelling his artistic fantasy.

Why does the transition from craftsmen's to artists' art not happen simultaneously in all artistic fields? Or in all parts of the world?

Example of irregularities in the development of art in different societies: until recently African craftsmen's art existed side-by-side with European artists' art. Now it is slowly turning into artists' art.

Example of temporal irregularities in the transition of craftsmen's to artists' art in different artistic spheres: in German literature this transition took place somewhat earlier than in German music. One of the key explanations is: the development of German literature was connected to the rise of a German-speaking, middle–class reading public. By contrast, the development of music in Mozart's time was decisively influenced by court taste. The fact that Mozart depended for his living on the court aristocracy while his personal make-up was already that of a freelance artist who sought primarily to follow the flow of his own imagination and the dictates of his own artistic conscience, was the most important reason for the tragedy of his life.

The psychological problem

Undoubtedly, the psychological problem cannot be dealt with separately from the sociological problem. What is involved is a process that has received practically no attention from academic psychologists and relatively little from psychoanalytical psychologists – the process of *sublimation*. I have pointed out provisionally that among the peculiarities of the non-courtly, 'freelance' artist is a combination of free-flowing fantasy with the ability to control this fantasy by individual self-restraint, by a highly developed conscience. More precisely: fantasy–streams and impulses of conscience are not merely reconciled within the framework of an artistic activity but are actually fused together. That is at the core of what we refer to as 'artistic genius'. The stream of fantasies and dreams is not only divested of the strongly animal tendencies at its root, which are unacceptable to the conscience stream; it actually releases its energy in harmony with the social canon without losing its spontaneity. Without purification by the artistic conscience the stream of dreams and fantasies is anarchistic and chaotic to all people except the dreamer. The libidinal fantasy–stream only becomes significant for other people, i.e. capable of mediation, if it is socialised through fusion with the canon, while at the same time energising and individualising the canon or the conscience. What is often called the 'sleepwalking certainty' with which great artists like Mozart so shape their fantasy material that one feels that the product could not be different, is an expression of this fusion of the fantasy–stream with the artistic conscience.

Act I: 27 January 1756 – September 1777

* Childhood and youth of a prodigy
* Father and son. The development of their relationship
* The fruitless search for posts at the courts of Europe
* Breaking of his voice (in Naples) and the increasing pressure of his father's dominance
* Mozart's unique musical training. Acquaintanceship with all the known and famous musicians of his time (including Johann Christian Bach, Gluck, Haydn, Johann Adolf Hasse,

Padre Martini). All this in addition to the intensive training by his father

Act II: September 1777 – 8 June 1781

* The first journey without his father. Beginning of emancipation and its difficulties: conscience
* The first (known) love affair: his cousin (Bäsle), Mozart's low woman
  The first (known) great love: Aloisia Weber, Mozart's higher woman – sex and eroticism
* The first (known) major quarrel with his father
* Mozart's faecal humour. Problem: what in this humour is characteristic of the canon of his society, and what is Mozartian, i.e. specifically individual? The problem of humour in relation to civilisation to be considered as an individual flight into ideas; constant linking of faecal and oral fantasies. Compulsive character which is nevertheless under control
* Growing awareness of his own value
* Growing awareness of his vocation as a composer, especially of operas: the first operas, initially rather imitative (including *La finta semplice*, 1768; *Mitridate*, 1770; *Lucio Silla*, 1772; *La finta giardiniera*, 1775); a large number of instrumental pieces: string quartets, divertimenti; the first G minor symphony (1773), violin concertos (1775)
* Return to Salzburg, appointment at the Salzburg court as leader of the orchestra and court organist (15 January 1779). In the same year: Goethe's *Iphigenie auf Tauris* (first version); Gluck's opera *Iphigenie auf Tauris*; Lessing, *Nathan der Weise*
* Performance of his last opera seria of this period, *Idomeneo* (Munich, 1780/1). Opera in the old style, but already with much individual development. Lessing, *Über die Erziehung des Menschengeschlechts*; Wieland, *Oberon*. Death of Empress Maria Theresa.
* Breach with the archbishop

Act III: 8 June 1781 – May 1788

The liberation of the artistic imagination, the individualisation of the canon. Court music in a unique, highly individualised form. To mention only operas: 16 July 1782, first performance of *Die Entführung aus dem Serail* ('Too many notes', says the emperor). First performance of Schiller's *Die Räuber*. 1 May 1786, *The Marriage of Figaro*; critical reception. 7 May 1788, *Don Giovanni*. Economy measures in Vienna owing to Turkish war.

Act IV: 1788 – 5 December 1791

Growing loneliness, increasing setbacks. If this act were represented dramatically, one would see Mozart standing on the stage while the people who have known him previously leave him one by one. His wife spends most of her time at baths, the noble/patrician pupils he had earlier (Countess Rumbeke, Countess Thun, Josepha Auernhammer, Theresa von Tracknern etc.) have all gone. Money worries and debts increase. The concert subscriptions he advertises fail completely. *Don Giovanni* is received coolly in Vienna, though warmly greeted in Prague. His letters show him in a state of increasing despair, partly because of his financial troubles, partly because of his psychological isolation.
The reasons are diverse:

* Rejection by court-aristocratic society in connection with *Figaro*, which was probably seen as seditious
* His works become increasingly difficult for the public to understand
* Composing increasingly for himself, following the pull of his own imagination. The three great symphonies and other works are produced without patrons, as a freelance artist. But as yet the institutions of a free market for musical works hardly exist

Two Notes

Do not forget Mozart's String Quintet in G minor (K 516): the agitated, almost tragic mood is followed very abruptly by an almost trivial, half jocular theme, as if he could not allow the agony and the pain to last, as if he had to suppress them with a light, rather shallow and clownish melody. Naturally, he returns to the agitated, tragic theme, but it never regains the abrupt, powerful effect it had at the start, when it suddenly broke in on the listener.

Wittgenstein said: Whereof one cannot speak, thereof one should remain silent.

I believe it could be said with equal justice: Whereof one cannot speak, thereafter one should seek.[1]

---

1 *Editor's note*: The first of these notes is in English in the original. The second is related to the Mozart material through the place where it was found (cf. Hildesheimer, *op. cit.*, p. 37).

Editor's Afterword

Norbert Elias died on 1 August 1990. He was unable to follow and supervise the preparation of the present book. But he did approve my suggestion of editing a book on Mozart (without any connection with the 'Mozart Year', 1991); he formulated the title himself, another sign that he had recognised the edition as his own work. However, the claim spread by the press that he had been writing this book up to the day of his death is no more than a legend in the vein of 'famous last words'. In reality, he never expressed the intention of picking up the work on Mozart again, as he had done with regard to many other projects.

The texts printed above, for the selection and final drafting of which I am responsible, were produced within the framework of a larger project, which also manifested itself in persistent announcements of the title *Der bürgerliche Künstler in der höfischen Gesellschaft* ('The bourgeois artist in court society') as volume 12 of the new series of the Suhrkamp edition of his works. The Elias Archive contains the following relevant material:

1. Untitled typescript (labelled 'Mozart') of 81 pages, partly with handwritten corrections and additions, together with preliminary drafts of some passages and uncompleted

additional notes. This text was very probably written in conjunction with Lecture 5.

2. Typescript 'Mozart in Vienna' (labelled 'Mozart Act IV'), 15 + 5 pages, with handwritten corrections in some places, also with some preliminary drafts and additional notes (see p. 130, n. 17). This text was probably written for a planned book on Mozart.

3. Typescript 'The bourgeois artist in court society as exemplified by Mozart' (labelled 'Artist'), 14 pages; possibly produced for another lecture not preserved in the Elias Archive.

4. Typescript 'Plan' (probably for 1 and/or 5), 6 pages.

5. Edited tape recording of a lecture (with discussion) given in Bielefeld at the invitation of the Faculty of Literature and Linguistics, with the title: 'Sociological reflections [problems] on genius as exemplified by Mozart'. The date of this lecture is difficult to establish at this stage, but is likely to have been in the winter term of 1978/9.

6. Edited tape recording and transcript of an extempore lecture broadcast on Westdeutscher Rundfunk III (published in a slightly edited and shortened form in *die tageszeitung*, 4 August 1990, p. 14).

7. Various typewritten and handwritten notes.

The present book was assembled from this material. Its three parts correspond essentially to Typescripts 1, 2 and 4 (with two notes from 7). Typescript 3 contains too many duplications of the other material to justify printing it separately. However, parts of it, some shorter and some longer, do contain new ideas and have been incorporated in the 'Sociological reflections on Mozart' and in some cases in notes. Lecture 5 and some of the notes from 7 have been used in the same way, while Lecture 6 yielded virtually no new material. All the longer extracts from other manuscripts found their place in the second and third chapters of the 'Reflections' (pp. 10–41 above). It also seemed advisable to enlarge and reorganise Typescript

1 in this way because Elias had originally approached his main sociological ideas on this subject rather tentatively.

In the first of the above texts all the titles and the breaks between chapters, sections and in some cases paragraphs are by the editor. The manuscript, which the author had not finalised, has been edited for publication (careful integrating and tightening of the argument, checking of facts, quotations and references, some attention to style). Apart from the material from other manuscripts already mentioned, excerpts from preliminary or additional notes, including an unfinished excursus from Typescript 2, have been incorporated. The procedure was similar with the second text, which was also divided up differently and supplemented by passages from additional notes in sections 3 and 4, although less condensation was needed. Minor deletions to avoid overlap with the first part were made only where this did not disrupt the context. The concluding Plan, which gives an idea of a possible outline of the book as envisaged by the author at a certain time, has been slightly shortened. The fact that the three texts printed cover broadly the same field was accepted as each does so on a different level of synthesis.

So much for the editor's report.

I shall conclude with some more personal comments. Since 1983 I have brought out on average one volume each year of mainly unpublished work by Norbert Elias, whether as editor, translator or in some informal function. This editorial project, through which Elias has been established as an author of contemporary relevance in Germany, has its origin in a personal initiative of mine, which I have been able to realise as a result of my own commitment and the invaluable help of others, especially Friedhelm Herborth (Suhrkamp Verlag) and Hermann Korte (University of Bochum). Title by title, I managed to circumvent Elias's dreadful ambivalence towards publication. Only someone who has had experience of this author as publisher's reader, editor or publisher, can have an idea of the tact, perseverance, enthusiasm and affection that the task demanded.

With regard to their substance, too, the volumes that came to be published in this way were the result of a curious form of collaboration on which I may report in more detail one day. Increasingly, a procedure emerged whereby I as the editor had the task of converting the rough drafts, fragments and even the isolated ideas of the author into rounded texts or finished books. This kind of communal effort demanded on my side a high degree of understanding, judgement, empathy and ability to shape the material, naturally without adding or subtracting anything on my own account. Where it seemed appropriate or was desired, I had to be ready to voice a direct opinion. On Elias's side the collaboration implied above all a unique degree of trust, which grew up as he was able to convince himself from a number of small-scale samples that I was able to perform such a task in the way he wished. One might sum up the arrangement by saying that Elias delegated a part of his over-strict conscience and his somewhat relaxed scrutiny of reality to me. I myself was willing (not without some struggle) to be used in this intimate way, as I had set myself the goal of bringing back this great Jewish writer from his exile to his former linguistic homeland. The result was books that were entirely by Elias and yet were 'ours', as Elias himself sometimes put it. All this had nothing to do with philology or the usual editorial morality, but a great deal to do with the real process of book production within a network of living people. Norbert Elias fully assented to this process – and this will remain one of the richest experiences of my life – because it corresponded deeply to his own image of the human being.

In working on *Mozart* I continued to use the same method, as if the death of the author had changed nothing. I believe now that this was an attempt to deny the death of a much loved old man. But in retrospect it is clear that my previous editorial procedure was tied to the personal relationship and cannot be simply transferred to the publication of a true posthumous *oeuvre*. For that a different institutional and perhaps a different methodological framework must be found. The present essay on the 'sociology of a genius', which tells so movingly of a father–son relationship and of the antagonistic intertwining of both parties' need for fulfilment, is my epitaph for a revered teacher and friend.

Berlin, 7 March 1991   Michael Schröter

Index